ARTISTS AT WORK

ARTISTS AT WORK BY BERNARD CHAET

WEBB BOOKS, INC. CAMBRIDGE, MASSACHUSETTS

Copyright © 1960 by Bernard Chaet

Library of Congress Catalog Card Number: 61-11079

Manufactured in the United States of America

Design: Norman S. Ives

CONTENTS

INTRODUCTION

This book is concerned with one aspect of works of art: materials and techniques. By means of discussion with painters, sculptors, draftsmen, and printmakers, through the examination of the methods used by certain earlier artists, and by talks with the manufacturers of materials, the author has attempted to cover the many different approaches to the artist's basic tools, with particular reference to those newly available to the contemporary artist. Problems met with by all the various workers in the different media are here discussed. The book is designed to provide information that will be helpful to the novice as well as suggestions that may serve as a jumping-off place for the more experienced worker who wishes to carry out his own experiments.

The author wishes at this point to add a word of warning. He does not intend to imply by his concern with materials and techniques that the studio should become a laboratory in which the artist is surrounded by paint specimens, chemicals, or machines. Such an approach would be as wrong as the picture of the artist as a totally free spirit, who wholly ignorant of his materials, can create on impulse works of art out of whatever lies at hand — even thin air. Briefly, the artist should know his materials; he must not make a fetish of them.

In general, the chapters that follow fall into three groups. In some, the very limitation of a technique has influenced the nature of the final work. In others, an artist has developed a traditional method for his own purposes. In the third group, new materials, developed by manufacturers, have made possible new effects.

Among those who work within limitations of a medium is the sculptor, Leonard Baskin, whose bronze casting in sand (technique) imposes limitations on the variety of forms. Yet Baskin's success is such that unless one is familiar with this technique on viewing his bronzes, awareness of these limitations never enters one's head. Similarly, the material from which Elbert Weinberg's bronze sculptures are originally constructed — long flat sheets of wax — has inspired his form ideas. Edouard Vuillard's painting medium — distemper — produced a special warmth in the earth colors and an acid brilliance in the greens and blues, which was appropriate for the effect he wanted. Josef Albers' oil technique is the simplest possible — the delivery of the paint directly from tube to support with a palette knife — yet the magic in his color combinations is such as to suggest a secret formula.

Among those who have expanded traditional methods is Panos Ghikas, who at first employed egg tempera in techniques prescribed by Cenini. But new visual concepts led him to devise new methods which yet do not violate the medium's characteristics. Esther Geller, working in the ancient medium of encaustic, was forced to invent formulas and procedures to make it workable for contemporary purposes. Conrad Marca-Relli's method of pasting canvas on canvas has enabled him to do mural-size collages, thereby changing the scale of what formerly was almost exclusively a miniature method. Hyman Bloom's "invention" of an ink made from Conte crayon dust and his use of water-soluble ink has made it possible for the artist to make changes in his work as it goes along, while still employing a technique that was previously noted for its direct permanency. Rudy Pozzatti's etching technique — that of dissolving hard ground with benzine instead of incising with an instrument — has made new effects possible, the method having been inspired by an image which traditional techniques could not achieve. Finally, Pat Adams' gouache technique — scraping, washing, burnishing — has expanded the possibilities of what has been considered a "sketch" medium.

The last twenty-five years have seen the introduction of many new methods and materials — perhaps more than any other period. New materials, originally created for industry, both have made traditional concepts easier to manage from a craft standpoint and inspired new experiments. Gabor Peterdi's paintings with Lucite plastic and oil reveal the tool marks (which he wished to preserve) that oil normally blurs. Lucite also aids James Brooks in achieving his rich interplay of opaque, translucent, and transparent areas. The new water soluble plastic resins have produced a whole range of technical possibilities, and they have made the old dream of both complete and fast drying a reality. Alfred Duca employs p.v.a. plastic to produce stained-glass effects. Karl Zerbe employs the same medium to construct with ease cement-like impastos; formerly this surface could only be produced by forcing another medium (oil) into an unnatural role. P.v.a. emulsion has also helped create permanent paper collages

(Irwin Rubin) and a new varnish for pastel (Ernest Boyer). Pastel and another plastic, polymer resin (or Rhoplex), has led to the creation of an interesting mixed technique by Arnold Bittleman. And two other young artists, George Lockwood and Arthur Hoener, stress the easy handling of this medium, which adapts itself so well to individual approaches.

In sculpture, Seymour Lipton's new organic imagery forced him to create a whole new direct metal technique. On the other hand, the form of Robert Engman's sculpture is based on the particular material he employs. In print-making, Edmund Casarella has worked with an ordinary material — cardboard — which he has transformed into a new print medium, permitting unlimited color printing. And in drawing, Al Blaustein's "play" with unorthodox tools such as lettering pens or soda straws has produced seemingly casual drawings of graphic power.

All of these inventions, new media, and experiments were activated by personal vision; the medium remains the medium — *that is, the transmitter of a concept. Technical virtuosity for the sake of "crafty" effects is not the concern of these artists. But, finally, the artist (in any medium) imagines his future work in terms of his technique or method or materials. The marriage of concept and technique is then complete. And every artist worthy of the name must become a master of his medium.*

I wish to thank Arts *for permission to reproduce many of these articles and to thank again all the artists who have made this book possible. I wish also to thank Dwight W. Webb, who had the idea for this volume and who helped greatly in the final editing.*

PART ONE: PAINTING

1.

Magic Formulas

Attitudes on Craft

In writing a book of this kind, one is constantly faced with the question: Are there magic formulas or media and surface treatments which in themselves make the difference between good and bad painting? And inevitably the second question follows: To what extent does a painter need a high degree of this kind of technical knowledge? There are almost as many answers to these two questions as there are painters and art experts, ranging from those whose emphasis is on craft knowledge, to those who totally reject the idea of a conscious approach to craft.

The first extreme position has been stated recently in a book *The Secret Formulas and Techniques of the Masters* by Jacques Maroger, former Technical Director of the Laboratory of the Louvre. After many years of search, Mr. Maroger claimed to have found the secret oil medium of the old masters — oil boiled with lead in various combinations. Lead acts as a dryer in this medium, which is commonly known as "black oil," since impurities in the oil turn it black on boiling. The virtues of the medium are that it produces a rapid-drying lustrous surface and that it offers many possibilities of formula variation, for the oil can be mixed with wax or emulsified with water. In his book, Mr. Maroger listed the formulas used by the following masters, Leonardo, Rubens, Titian, and Rembrandt, and the implication is left that the artist-reader can simply take his choice. For example, Rembrandt's medium is described as the addition of a "maximum quantity of wax in the impasto." And, in fact, there are many painters — including Raoul Dufy — who have read Mr. Maroger's work and made use of this "secret."

Other authorities as well have been concerned with old-master media, particularly that of Rembrandt. In *The Artist at Work,* H. Ruhemann, a restorer at London's National Gallery where a number of Rembrandts were recently cleaned, states — in opposition to Mr. Maroger — that the pre-eighteenth-century masters, including Rembrandt, "could not have used any appreciable proportion of soft resin or wax." In fact, there is no unanimous opinion among experts as to the nature of Rembrandt's medium: Professor A. P. Laurie has suggested that the secret was the use of stand oil; Max Doerner, Venice turpentine, mastic varnish, and sun-thickened oil; but scientists have not as yet been able to verify any of these conjectures. Even if we assume that more accurate analysis of such media will disclose the actual constituents employed, the question remains: How much influence will this discovery have on painters and their crafts?

Mr. Morager made an attempt to answer this question. He stated that the secrets which he had rediscovered were lost towards the end of the eighteenth century and, from this fact, drew the conclusion that, "The decadence that followed was inevitable, and a certain drama lies in the fact that this decadence was due simply to the loss of a secret technique — that is to say, to a cause that was entirely material." And he summed up his case as follows: "But only the knowledge of technical means, which he had lacked until this day, will enable the painter of tomorrow to take part successfully in the many still unknown possibilities."

Experts have proposed other magic formulas, one of the most popular today being concern with texture to the exclusion of different painterly qualities. Those who hold this point of view believe a heavily textured canvas to be the most important feature in contemporary expression, as if the emphasis on impasto would, in itself, guarantee "quality" or "richness" in the painting.

The view most diametrically opposed to that of Mr. Maroger is held by a number of contemporary painters, who have reacted violently against technical formulas of all kinds. Some of these artists have deliberately abandoned "sound practice" and have chosen to paint with the quickest and cheapest materials available. For these painters, the permanence of their works is irrelevant. One often hears the statement: "I would rather paint a good picture that falls apart than a bad one that lasts forever." One cannot quarrel with such a remark, but one may wonder if it meets the problem any more successfully than Mr. Maroger's obsession with magic formulas.

It is true that an exaggerated concern with techniques may lead to a sterile approach. The painter, restricted to his belief that the choice of medium and other didactic rules are the key to mastery, unwittingly depreciates his own visual realization. He catalogues painters according to their craft alone. For the zealot of this viewpoint, Cezanne becomes simply the man whose paint cracked when he used too much Prussian blue.

Similarly, preoccupation with textural quality can lead one to hold that Rembrandt's surface, rather than his plastic, inventions are the key to his genius. Or it implies what is impossible to assume — that Van Gogh first invented his brush and then trusted inspiration to put it to use. The "texture school," if we may call it such, tends to forget that every painter accommodated the individual surface of his canvases to an original plastic concept. In short, the concept has found the textural means to express itself.

The other extreme — the belief that technical knowledge in itself hampers expression — also is untenable. Painters who take this point of view apparently forget that the term "painter" itself implies knowledge of a craft and of the nature of materials, their characteristics, and their permanence. (Here it may be added, parenthetically, that over any period of time permanent materials are more economical.) We must also keep in mind that if the painter has a responsibility to his collector, matters of craft must be part of his concern. Paintings that crack, warp, or otherwise deteriorate hardly inspire confidence. But, most of all, we feel that this anti-craft attitude has emerged as a reaction against the mystery that has been made of technical practice. The notion that simple technical knowledge (permanent media, color, grounds, supports) is so difficult to obtain that its acquisition will be frustrating should be dispelled.

Actually, there are many examples of the close interrelation between freshness of creative impulse and a new utilization of traditional techniques or materials. Max Beckmann, for example, often underpainted in pastel. For Marca-Relli the edge of the pasted canvas created a simultaneous line giving the spatial tension no other means could achieve.

Similarly, the unusual tool can implement the expression of the concept. Arshile Gorky found a sign writer's long-haired brush a means to satisfy his calligraphic ideas. Pollock perforated paint cans, the fluid line being produced by the escaping liquid. Arthur Osver has found a dental tool useful for gently exposing colors beneath the top layer of paint.

As can be guessed from the above, the writer of this book believes that the pitfalls of both extreme positions can be avoided. To those who yearn for the secrets of the old masters he would mention that over twenty new colors, produced today, were unknown before the eighteenth century, and yet he would insist that it would be ridiculous to argue that the existence of these colors makes contemporary art superior to that of the previous centuries. To the painter, fearful of craft knowledge, he would say that it is time we realized that the concepts of the painter as genius and of the painter as craftsman are not in the least incompatible. Thorough knowledge of craft is neither inhibiting nor is it in itself — without the other necessary gifts — a guarantee of achievement. At its best, mastery of craft is a vocabulary, one that opens possibilities which may be fulfilled by the individual vision of the artist.

Van Gogh: Here texture is in the service of the plastic concept.

Edouard Vuillard, French, 1868-1940: *Under the Trees*. 1894.
Distemper on canvas, 84½ x 38½". The Cleveland Museum of Art. Gift
of Hanna Fund.

2.   Potentialities of Distemper

Edouard Vuillard

The term "distemper" refers to size or glue color painting. Velas-quez's teacher, Pacheco, noted that the old masters used distemper exclusively for preliminary exercises and, according to Max Doerner, there is evidence that distemper may have been used for wall painting in Pompeii. Today we are most apt to come upon distemper in connection with Edouard Vuillard. In his mid-twenties Vuillard designed and painted a number of the-atrical sets; he began to use distemper about the same time, and it is probable that he discovered this fast-drying medium in the theater. In any event, he afterwards employed distemper (alter-nately with oil) throughout his career. Unlike most painters, who use water media only for small paintings, Vuillard utilized distemper for his largest works. At times he used it on board and paper, but mostly on canvas.

A painter chooses his medium to aid his vision but his vision, in turn, must then adapt itself to the medium, and each medium has its advantages and disadvantages. Distemper has its peculiar difficulties (although Vuillard made it look easy). It will not blend like oil; if made improperly it becomes sticky and, if it spoils, the smell is unbearable. Textural effects are limited; glue is fairly brittle and cannot be built into a heavy impasto. On the other hand, it does have its definite advantages. The ingredients, rabbitskin glue or gelatin, are relatively inexpensive; they dry rapidly, almost immediately; one does not have to think about slow and fast-drying colors. Color is mat and brilliant, oil colors being relatively darker because of the oil's shine. Blues and greens, which are dulled in oil, are especially brilliant in dis-temper, while the warm earth colors glow. Naturally, Vuillard took full advantage of the visual sensations inherent in the medium.

André Gide, reviewing the Salon d'Automne in 1905, wrote of Vuillard, "He explains each color by its neighbor and obtains from both a reciprocal response." The building of brushstrokes into magical color shapes and interspaces was Vuillard's style. He did not often blend, even in oil. The warm energy of his ochers and umbers, employed in harmony or dissonance with vibrating greens and blues, springs from his natural use of this particular medium. (In contrast, some painters spend a great deal of time trying to make oil look like fresco.) In short, distemper was natural for his method of applying pigments, and natural for his color ideas.

There are few published recipes for making distemper, and most of those that do exist are vague: "Take some thick glue size and thin with water to desired consistency." But in the past eight years experimentation at Yale has made possible certain definite recommendations. George Lockwood, a young New York painter who studied at Yale, has been instrumental in this research, and some of the following measurements are his. First, as for the glue itself, two kinds are possible — rabbitskin glue (Grumbacher or Permanent Pigments) or gelatin (Grumbacher). Rabbitskin glue (ten to twelve parts of water to one part of crushed glue by volume) is placed in a pan. If gelatin is used, make the proportion fifteen to one by volume. This mixture is soaked in a pan for an hour; soaking longer does not change any of the results. Heat the contents in a double boiler, stirring constantly. When the glue is completely dissolved, the medium is prepared. The glue should never be allowed to boil, for boiling destroys its glue action. Distemper is easier to apply when warm; the glue gels as it cools, making it hard to handle. But this does not mean that the glue must be kept constantly on the stove; a pan of hot water will serve to keep it warm, and in hot weather the last procedure is unnecessary. Experimentation has shown that, once the medium has been prepared, thinning with additional water is dangerous; the glue mixture must be kept consistent. Moreover, to insure freshness the medium should be made new daily. Finally, there is some difference in handling between the two glues discussed; Mr. Lockwood found that gelatin sets more rapidly, is more transparent, and is more apt to show the individual brushstroke.

The colors employed are dry pigments (Fezandie and Sperrle, 205 Fulton St., New York City). It is not easy to answer the question of how much medium to use for each pigment. Pacheco, writing about egg tempera, noted that fluffy pigments require more medium than heavier ones. This observation also applies to distemper. For example, alizarin or Hansa yellow requires more medium than the earth colors. Preliminary tests should be made by the individual painter. Insufficient medium will cause flaking and will leave the painting excessively water-soluble.

Heavy rag paper makes an excellent support. Dampen the paper and tape it to a board. When dry it can be sized with the medium. Sizing is recommended if the natural color of the paper is to be exposed; it increases evenness of adherence. Distemper paintings on paper are flexible enough to be rolled without cracking. A gesso panel also makes an excellent support and ground. One should make sure that the gesso is prepared with the same glue as the medium; a foreign glue may prevent the original glue from really sticking to the panel. And finally, although canvas may be used, a commercially prepared oil-ground canvas is not suitable; oil grounds and tempera medium are not compatible. Unprepared linen (Utrecht Linens) is best. First, the linen should be stretched; second, it should be sized with the medium. If a ground color is desired, it must be applied as a second coat with the medium and dry pigments.

A final spray with 4% formalin solution protects the painting from bacteria and makes it insoluble in water. Polymer Tempera (see page 31) has also been found to be a suitable varnish. Polymer may turn milky after being sprayed, but a gentle heating over a radiator, or with a heat lamp, makes it completely invisible. Other varnishes, however, have been found to destroy the desired matness of the distemper medium.

A final note: in addition to its brilliant mat color, its fast-drying advantages, and its comparatively low cost, distemper makes an excellent underpainting for oil.

Panos Ghikas: *Abstraction No. I, 1948*. Egg Tempera. 12 x 15″.

3.   Egg Tempera Transformed

Panos Ghikas

How far can a painting medium be stretched to imitate the surface of another medium? Can oil be flattened to produce the optical mat brilliance of tempera? Or the reverse? Panos Ghikas, a practitioner in both oil and tempera, who discussed this problem with the author believes that oil which is forced into a mat surface negates the medium's natural shine. This imitation of tempera, he said, is a misapplication of the medium's beauty; Leger to his mind is a case in point. Championing the "natural use" of a particular medium, Mr. Ghikas pointed out "that a plastic idea can change the use of the medium but cannot change its inherent characteristics." He illustrated this thesis with his two egg-tempera paintings here reproduced.

The earlier painting represents the more traditional approach to egg tempera. The modeling from light to dark through cross-hatching relates to the Florentine formula. According to Mr. Ghikas, "the method was a way of fusing this traditionally brittle medium, thereby making it seem more elastic." For Mr. Ghikas this cross-hatching represented the solution of earlier form problems which produced a purely black and white graphic solution. "It forced," he remarked, "an interest in 'handwriting for its own sake.' Of course, in the hands of a master like Sassetta it became a delicate personal handwriting. In a less versatile painter it was apt to become a mechanical procedure." In Mr. Ghikas' own development, this method became increasingly

difficult to use as he evolved a more personal plastic mode. Therefore, his problem was to change the use of tempera without
changing its characteristics.

The second reproduction illustrates the profound change
which appeared in his work. To put it simply, his new preoccupation was the interaction of color and shape to create space.
To do this he used geometric space-illusion as well as overlapping
of shapes. Color was used in its pure state for the most part, with
a color changing its appearance by use of different undercoats.
For example, a cadmium yellow over a white had a different
"weight" than over another yellow. Mr. Ghikas clarifies this
point in the following words: "This changing of the depth of
tone can give the illusion of transparency to this essentially
opaque medium. Dense opacity was built by five thin washes of
the same color, whereas this illusion of a glaze was produced by
a white underpainting with a few coats of yellow." In this manner Mr. Ghikas found that he could "change" an individual
color and thereby influence those that surround it. The transfer

Panos Ghikas: *Macdowell Colony No. I.* Egg Tempera, 5 x 21″. Collection Robert Graham.

from one visual mode to another could be achieved by one who intimately knew his medium.

Next, the conversation turned to Mr. Ghikas's materials. He used Weber dry pigments ground in water, his palette consisting of Permalba white, ivory black, chromium oxide, terre verte, viridian, alizarin, Chinese vermilion, cadmium yellow medium, Indian red, light red, and the various ochers, siennas, and umbers. The medium was egg yolk to which approximately one-eighth cold water by volume was added. Preservatives were not used to keep this mixture from spoiling; instead the pure mixture was stored in a refrigerator — a week is the maximum safe time. After that the binding properties of the egg may be destroyed. This medium may be thinned up to 50% with water: adding more water than that would endanger its properties.

For support, Mr. Ghikas used tempered Masonite; his ground was the traditional gesso of from eight to ten coats. A step-by-step description of the preparation of the ground is supplied by Mr. Ghikas: First the board is sanded to insure adhesion of the gesso. Then a thin coat of gelatin or rabbitskin glue (one part glue to sixteen parts water) was applied to both sides of the masonite. The gesso itself consisted of this glue water and whiting — two parts of whiting to one part of water. Sanding of the gessoed surfaces completed the ground.

Sable brushes were employed in both paintings, with one difference: the newer, flatter forms demanded unpointed brushes. Mr. Ghikas found worn sables ideal, for their broader bases covered larger areas and they left no trace of their strokes. Handling of the medium also differed: in his new paintings less water was used — in fact, an almost dry-brush effect was employed. These, then, worn unpointed brushes and less thinning with water represent the major changes in the actual use of materials, and yet the appearance of the paintings is distinctly different. Mr. Ghikas prefers the newer painting for more than technical reasons. His newer forms, he feels, are more economical in effect: "Tedious, mechanical procedure has been replaced with direct, immediate impact."

The transformation of an ancient medium to meet an individual need is a common experience for creative artists in all traditions. Under the influence of new plastic ideas, the painter must alter these inherited tools to make them accommodate his individual concepts. The painter who transforms his medium is the painter who knows it best.

––––––––––

Born in Malden, Mass., in 1924, PANOS GHIKAS *studied at Yale University School of Fine Arts and with Willi Baumeister at Staatliche Akademie der Bildenen Kunst in Stuttgart. He is now teaching at the School of the Boston Museum of Fine Arts. A McDowell Fellow, Mr. Ghikas has exhibited in a one-man show at the Margaret Brown Gallery in Boston and in group shows at the Art Institute of Chicago, Institute of Contemporary Art in Boston, and the University of Illinois. He is represented by the Graham Gallery in New York, and by the Kanegis Gallery in Boston.*

4.   P.V.A. Emulsion Tempera

Alfred Duca

One of the first artists to explore the possibilities of plastics for painting was Alfred Duca. His initial experiments in 1945 with p.v.a. (polyvinyl acetate) emulsions (water-thinned) were prompted by a desire to achieve a variety of surface textures, which was, at best, difficult and time consuming in oil. He was searching, too, for a stained glass luminosity and the obvious advantages of fast and complete drying of heavy layers of paint. Duca's efforts were complicated by two major technical problems. First, the available p.v.a. solutions, which mixed readily with pigments, contained a high percentage of acid which could "burn" such pigments as cobalt and ultramarine, as well as do damage to the ground and support. The acid problem was solved when Duca encouraged a sympathetic industrial chemist at a division of Borden's to produce a highly polymerized grade of p.v.a. which would be relatively acid free. The second problem was to make this milky-white bland solution dry in an absolutely clear state so that pigments were not grayed or stained. He experimented with the addition of various commercial plasticizers which would make the film continuous, that is, continuously transparent. Although this investigation by trial and error was time-consuming, he eventually selected the desired plasticizer from the many that were available, and determined the correct proportion of plasticizer to synthetic resin. To test this formula, Polymer Tempera (produced by Polymer Tempera, Inc., 17 Hawkins St. Somerville, Mass.), against the average p.v.a. solution, which comes in a familiar plastic bottle and is sold as a

Alfred Duca: *The Carob Tree*. Polymer Tempera 55 x 36″.

glue, spread them both out on a glass, permit them to dry thoroughly, and notice the difference in clarity.

Duca's research resulted in a new medium with the possibilities of new aesthetic attitudes as its normal by-product. His work became a stimulus to other painters to experiment with the new polymerized plastic resin emulsions — both p.v.a. and acrylic. And in addition, this new medium was also a great aid to those painters working in collage (page 69) who demanded a permanent, strong, colorless glue which would not damage paper or canvas.

P.v.a. polymer may be mixed directly with dry pigments on the palette (glass) immediately before application. It is not necessary to grind the pigments thoroughly with the medium as in oil for the medium's strong glue action completely encases the color. Some painters prefer to grind pigments with water into a paste and store them in sealed jars until ready for use. However, mixtures of color and p.v.a. cannot be stored because of the quick hardening qualities of the medium. All water soluble tube colors such as casein, gouache, or water colors are compatible with the medium and may be used directly with the medium or added to the dry pigments and medium mix. Colors are mixed on the palette in roughly one-third pigment to two-thirds medium; roughly because each pigment inherently requires a different proportion of binder (see quote from Pacheco, page 25). Fluffy pigments, such as alizarin or Hansa yellow which are difficult to "wet," require more medium. A few drops of denatured alcohol added to the mix is an aid in controlling difficult pigments. To test the picture for flaking caused by insufficient medium, scratch gently with a palette knife or touch with a damp cloth — the painting should not wipe or scratch off. Web-like cracks are also a sign that insufficient medium has been employed. But Duca notes that most painters who employ p.v.a. tend to use too much medium. "They do not realize," he stresses, "that the medium can be thinned out almost 50% with water and still retain satisfactory adhesion."

The milkiness of the medium which appears to discolor the

pigments when they are mixed together on the palette disappears on drying. But in cold weather a clouded film may appear on the surface. A gentle heating with a heat lamp or holding the picture over a radiator will dissolve the whiteness. Extreme cold will destroy the liquid medium itself — it must be kept from freezing — and metal, tin, or galvanized containers must be avoided because they will discolor it.

Depending on the amount of polymer medium that is mixed with the colors, the surface will be glossy or mat. The less one thins with water, the shinier the surface. Duca's paintings normally possess a rich shiney surface built up of luminous glazes. He further intensifies the shine by varnishing with denatured alcohol; one must varnish quickly in order not to disturb the film. By contrast, Karl Zerbe's paintings in the same medium are painted directly with flat opaque mixtures. He extends the paint with inert ingredients, such as powdered clay, to form thick buttery pastes; the addition of such materials causes little loss of color brilliance. Ultimately, the surfaces of Zerbe's paintings come to resemble fresco. The p.v.a. medium, then, can be used in a water-thin solution or it can be used to build up considerable thicknesses without danger. Layers of paint can be applied over old layers without danger for they all fuse into one mass.

According to Duca, the emulsion has not yellowed, darkened, or cracked during extensive tests, but it is perhaps too brittle a medium (due again to the strong glue action) to apply to canvas without very special care. Panels of untempered Masonite make a safe support. However, canvas or muslin may be glued to the board. A ground solution of one part medium to two parts water may be brushed on the Masonite before dampened canvas is stretched over it. Another coat of solution is then applied. Heavy paper or cardboard may be employed as a support for medium extensively diluted with water. (P.v.a. makes a water color water-proof.)

Polymer gesso may also be applied to a panel with or without the canvas cover. Equal amounts of zinc white powder (or titanium) and whiting are mixed with a 50-50 solution of water

Karl Zerbe: *Red Clown*, 1956, Polymer Tempera, 39 x 29". Collection Allan Sirotto.

and medium; the proportion is two parts dry mixture to one part diluted medium. The back of a panel should also be gessoed to prevent warping.

Varnishing is not necessary, but varnishing with alcohol, as mentioned, will shine the surface. A wax paste (beeswax dissolved in warm turpentine) may be applied to give a consistent finish if shiny spots appear due to many variations of the water to resin proportion (the proportion of medium to water should be kept constant to prevent this from occurring). Lastly, the medium itself can be used as a varnish (see pastel, page 42). In using p.v.a., special care must be taken of brushes; otherwise the medium is particularly destructive. They should be wet with water before painting and cleaned with soap and water afterward, and it is advisable to keep them immersed in water if the painting procedure is interrupted. Nylon brushes which can be purchased at house-paint outlets are recommended both for p.v.a. and Rhoplex; they seem to withstand the plastics better than average artists' brushes.

To sum up, polyvinyl acetate tempera emulsion lends itself to many different handling possibilities. It resembles natural emulsion temperas such as distemper and egg in that the colors dry out lighter than they appear in the wet state, and the painter must learn to visualize the final effect. But the possibilities of building heavy impastos, plus the possibilities of infinite glazing coupled with fast drying and the complete fusing of each coat onto the last, give this new medium potentialities that cannot be found in any other material.

ALFRED DUCA *was born in Boston in 1920. He studied with Alexander Kostellow (Pratt Institute) and Karl Zerbe (School of the Boston Museum of Fine Arts), and has taught children's classes at Boys Clubs of Boston. His exhibits include one-man shows at Boris Mirski Gallery and De Cordova Museum in Lincoln, Mass. Winner of a Rockefeller grant in sculpture, Mr. Duca's work is in collections of the Addison Gallery, Worcester Museum, Brandeis University, and the Munson-Williams-Procter Institute. Mr. Duca is represented by Boris Mirski Gallery.*

KARL ZERBE, *born in Berlin in 1903, attended the Debschitz Art School and the Munich Academy. He emigrated to the U. S. A. in 1934, settling in Boston. For seventeen years, he was head of the Department of Painting in the Boston Museum School, and now holds a similar position at Florida State U. He has had numerous one-man shows, and is represented in many major museums, including the Whitney, Phillips Gallery, Detroit Institute, and the Philadelphia Museum. The Nordness Gallery is his representative in New York; Boris Mirski, in Boston.*

5. Rhoplex Emulsion Tempera

Experiment by Young Artists

Studio-laboratory experts warn painters that the new plastics developed for industrial use are not time-tested and therefore unsafe for artists' use. Yet, if painters do not dare to experiment with these materials, how are we to measure their ultimate worth? Furthermore, when a new product with unique qualities appears, can it not, in some ways, aid creation?

The search for new materials is aided by chemical firms which are willing to send samples to artists. Some time ago Arthur Hoener was sent a sample of Rhoplex AC-33,* an acrylic-resin emulsion produced originally for water-base house paints. Mr. Hoener in turn dispensed portions to a trio of friends so that they might compare results. It should be noted that these painters were already working with water-base media such as casein, distemper, and Polymer Tempera, and they all possessed a wide range of dry pigments necessary for a tempera vehicle such as Rhoplex. The following is an extract from their discussion, which took place after six weeks of experimentation.

Arthur Hoener briefly outlined the product's background: "Rhoplex has been tested for several years by the housepainting industry; its sealing properties, color retention, film life, and adhesive power were all considered excellent." He catalogued associated products which can control and change the handling of the medium: Rhoplex B-85* is a hardening agent which makes the emulsion firmer and more brittle, and Tamol-731* is a

---

*Products of Rohm and Haas Company, Washington Square Resinous Products Division, Philadelphia 5, Pennsylvania

pigment-dispersing agent which prevents aggregates from forming. After this introduction the group (Louis LoMonaco, Paul Zelanski, George Lockwood, and Arthur Hoener) quickly agreed on the medium's outstanding characteristic — flexibility. In practice, the medium was found flexible enough to use on canvas or paper. Once the paint was applied to canvas — the unprimed canvas having been sized with the medium itself or the traditional rabbitskin glue — it was virtually impossible to crack the film. Oil paint cannot withstand such treatment.

Next, Louis LoMonaco compared Rhoplex to other temperas. He felt that Rhoplex, which possesses all the inherent qualities of tempera (fast-drying, with flat and opaque color), also had qualities which were unique. "This medium when thinned with water has glazing qualities comparable to oil. Further, Rhoplex does not resist the brush; it seems to have some of the fluid application of oil paint. This combination of tempera and oil effects offers unlimited handling possibilities to individual painters."

At this point Arthur Hoener mentioned a shortcoming of Rhoplex. Its use tends to limit textural effects: a relatively heavy impasto cannot be applied directly but has to be built up gradually, in layers. He pointed out that Polymer Tempera, a more brittle material, was more suited to direct impasto painting. "Yet," he added, "individual brush strokes can be exposed in Rhoplex, thereby creating texture." But most important to Hoener is that Rhoplex can be used as an underpainting for oil. "Oil with Lucite (see page 55), also an acrylic resin, produces a strong bond between the oil and the tempera. This is due, I believe, to the inherent strong adhesive qualities of Lucite, plus the added advantage of having a strong cohesive bond of the acrylics."

Paul Zelanski next outlined his method. He grinds pigments with Rhoplex and stores them in jars. "I use a one-to-one mixture of Rhoplex AC-33 and water with an addition of 5% Tamol as the grinding vehicle. Storing prepared colors in jars makes it possible for me to match colors when I repaint and retouch.

George Lockwood: *Insects in Flight*, 1957. Rhoplex Emulsion Tempera, 52″ high.

Arthur Hoener: *Emerging Spring*, 1958. Rhoplex Emulsion Tempera under-painting on canvas — overpainted with oil paint and Lucite 45.

This is important in tempera because colors appear lighter when they dry and it is difficult to remix the same colors." Mr. Zelanski felt that the addition of Tamol-731, the dispersing agent, keeps the surface even; unwanted lumpy surfaces produced by relatively unground pigments do not appear at random intervals, but are evenly dispersed in the medium. "And," he added, "traditionally difficult pigments behave themselves with Tamol."

George Lockwood's formula is the same except for the addition of a 20% solution of Rhoplex B-85, the hardening agent; he preferred a more brittle medium even though he paints on rag paper. He was principally attracted by Rhoplex's glazing potential and by its waterproof surface which makes it possible to do waterproof water colors and gouaches. He thought that other temperas were not as waterproof as Rhoplex. For example, he found that Rhoplex is difficult to remove even after prolonged soaking in water; only toluene or xylene will remove the film. He also praised Rhoplex's consistent drying — without shiny or dull spots.

Rhoplex acrylic emulsion, which has some of the handling qualities of oil paint as well as those of tempera, has an additional characteristic that should be noted. As in p.v.a. emulsion, one does not have to be concerned about fast- and slow-drying colors or a gradual fat-over-lean build-up of paints. It may be employed with pastel (see page 47) or as an under-painting for oil.

Obviously, Rhoplex is a medium which should attract a great many painters. When asked if their experiments involved only technical research, the members of the group assured the author that the possibilities of this unique medium added to their visual vocabulary. In fact, they stressed that they were already mentally composing in terms of the medium's wide range.

A native of New Jersey, ARTHUR HOENER *attended Cooper Union, the Brooklyn Museum School, and Hans Hofman School of Fine Art, before taking the degrees of B.F.A. and M.F.A. at Yale. He has exhibited widely throughout the country, having had one-man shows in New York in 1957, and in Boston in 1957 and 1960. At present, he is an Assistant Professor of Art at Boston U.*

GEORGE LOCKWOOD, *born in Brooklyn in 1929, studied at Cooper Union, the New School for Social Research, and Yale University. He now teaches graphics at the Massachusetts College of Art. His work is in many collections, including the Library of Congress, Yale University, and the Boston Museum. He is also the proprietor of a graphic workshop in Boston.*

6.   Pastel

Ernest Boyer

Degas and Redon are usually credited with transforming pastel into a major medium. More recently, Picasso, Klee, and Miró have employed pastel occasionally, and Max Beckman often used it for underpainting. If one is more apt to find pastel today among standard materials in artists' studios, the reason may be a new interest in color plus the compatibility of pastel with water-base paints.

Pure color is perhaps best symbolized by the brilliance of dry pigment. This near-spectrum brilliance is an exciting visual experience — which in practice is usually followed by complaints about the change in the color after the pigment has been ground with binding media. But, while wetting dry pigments cuts down their optical intensity, pastel offers the painter the same brilliance as the original pigment itself.

The relatively dry surfaces of casein, distemper, and some new plastic temperas make it possible to incorporate them with pastel without a visual separation caused by contrast of surface shine. By placing one medium over another, one can gain almost immediately a finished effect. Degas, for example, employed pastel in this manner with gouache, water color, and oil paint thinned with turpentine. He built glazelike surfaces by spraying fixative in between layers of pastel and paint. His technique also included spraying a pastel painting with hot water and working on it in the wet state with a brush. And on occasion he soaked his pastel sticks in steam to produce impasto-like effects. Degas's experiments transformed pastel into a medium which had the depth and translucence of oil paint. Redon, on the other hand, preferred a more direct application which dramatized the intensity of individual pigments.

Today, commercial pastels are adequate, but painters who desire a special range of color and a guarantee of permanence blend and manufacture their own pastel sticks. Such an artist is Ernest Boyer, who explained the following procedure when the author visited his studio, where Mr. Boyer was experimenting with grounds and fixatives as well as the manufacture of pastel. The color potential provided the original impulse which induced Boyer to experiment with pastel. He consulted Ralph Mayer's book* for formulas (It should be noted that this work is perhaps the most important technical book in use today). Here he found that the materials other than dry pigments required for making pastel include a mortar and pestle for grinding, gum tragacanth as a binder, beta naphthol as a preservative, and precipitated chalk as filler. Boyer followed these directions in Mayer's book:

> Pour a pint of water on about ⅓ ounce of gum tragacanth, cover the vessel and allow to stand overnight in a warm place. To the resulting gelatinous mass add a little beta naphthol to prevent it from spoiling. Label this solution A. Dilute a portion of it with one part water, labeling this solution B, and another portion with three parts of water, labeling this solution C. The various pigments will require solutions of different strengths to produce crayons of the proper degree of softness; very few will need the full strength A solution. Because of the variations in raw materials, no accurate instructions can be given for the amounts of binder necessary to make pastels of the proper texture.

Boyer's pastel sticks consisted of approximately two ounces of pigment. Dry pigments with a sufficient amount of binder were mixed in the mortar, rolled into sticks, and allowed to dry. He made the following sticks with the various solutions: viridian — A; cadmium red light, medium, dark, and manganese violet — A

---

*The Artists Handbook of Materials and Techniques, revised edition (Viking Press, New York, 1957).

Edgar Degas, French, 1834-1917: *Danseuses Roses* Pastel. Museum of Fine Arts, Boston.

and B; terre rose, ultramarine and chrome green oxide — B; cadmium yellow medium and deep — A and C; cadmium orange — B and C. White consisted of 80% precipitated chalk and 20% of titanium white with solution C. In addition he premixed the following: one part manganese violet and two parts white — B and C; one part manganese violet and three parts white — C; one part cadmium red light and three parts white — B and C; equal parts of cadmium red light, manganese violet, and white — B and C; equal parts of cadmium yellow deep and chrome green oxide — A and B; and ultramarine — B and C. Certain dry pigments are poisonous and should be avoided: emerald green, cobalt violet, and all lead colors.

Boyer experimented with various supports of Masonite, canvas, and paper. Paper with a certain degree of roughness or "tooth" is necessary to aid adherence. Commercially prepared toned papers were readily available, but Boyer preferred parchment paper which he sanded lightly with emery paper. Unsized linen glued to Masonite as well as gesso over muslin (again glued to Masonite) were also employed. Each of these supports and grounds produced a different surface texture.

Boyer's experiments also included several fixatives. Two in particular were recommended: Polymer Tempera thinned with five parts of water produced a fast-drying coating. A formula for a slower-drying fixative was found in Mayer's book. It consisted of one half ounce of fresh casein, one-fourth teaspoon pure ammonia, and one-half pint of pure grain alcohol. The fixative was prepared by soaking the casein in five ounces of water for about six hours and adding the ammonia drop by drop, stirring constantly. Alcohol was added, with more stirring, when the casein dissolved into a "heavy syrupy mass." Both the above fixatives were sprayed with an atomizer. Fixatives do, of course, change the color and must be used sparingly. A pastel may be framed without "fixing" by placing narrow strips of wood between the glass and the painting.

These technical experiments were inspired by possibilities of intense color which, combined with its other advantages (rapid execution and compatibility with water paints), make pastel a medium that is being encountered more frequently today.

ERNEST BOYER *was twenty-one years old when he was chosen to be represented in the U.S.I.S. International traveling group show of 1955-59. He has also exhibited at the Kalla Gallery in Pittsburgh. Born in Dayton, Ohio, in 1934, Mr. Boyer studied at Carnegie Institute of Technology and Yale University School of Art and Architecture.*

Arnold Bittleman: *Under the Wave*. Pastel and Rhoplex Tempera Emulsion.

7. Pastel and Rhoplex: a mixed technique
Arnold Bittleman

The prolonged drying time of oil colors has led many artists to experiment with faster-drying media. Casein and egg-emulsion tempera, as well as several new plastic temperas, are very much in evidence. Further, lacquers, enamels, and house paints to which drying agents are added have gained the favor of many painters in recent years. But as already noted sticks of pastel offer the swiftest possible application of pigment to support.

Arnold Bittleman, who in an interview outlined his methods and views to the author, employs pastel and Rhoplex AC-33, a plastic tempera (see page 37), in combination with dry pigments in an original mixed technique.

Bittleman works on a generous scale, employing rag paper as a support. The Arthur Brown Co. of New York is the source for the paper, which comes in rolls and is forty-two inches wide. A sheet of this paper, slightly dampened, is attached to Masonite with paper tape. Bittleman is careful not to stretch it too tightly since periodic spraying with plastic shrinks the paper, which may split or tear. After the paper is fastened to the board Bittleman begins a painting in one of three ways: he may arrange simple color patches with pastel and spray with Rhoplex; or he may cover the paper with one color by brushing on a mixture of Rhoplex and pigment; or, lastly, he may cover the paper with Liquitex gesso (a Rhoplex product of Permanent Pigments). This provides a toothy, slightly rough surface.

Let us trace the development of *Under the Wave,* reproduced here. Working with Rhoplex thinned with water and mixed with dry pigments, Bittleman covered the top of the paper with a light blue wash and gradually darkened the blue as he approached the bottom. Next, with the broad sides of pastel sticks, he developed a grouping of broad areas of pure unmodulated color. When the interaction of these color shapes satisfied him, he sprayed the entire painting with an equal mixture of Rhoplex and water to which he added a little whiting to preserve the mat surface. The spraying was accomplished with a Paasche Air Drive spray gun.

In a sense this first stage, of color areas, was close to what the viewer now sees at a distance when the painting is complete — but more about reading distances later. When the painting, in this first stage, was protected by the transparent film of plastic, Bittleman "drew" or scratched the surface with a sharp wood-cutting knife, disclosing the blue underneath. Bittleman emphasized that "these tool marks were not intended to produce texture but rather to articulate each individual form within the large masses." He continued, "Nor is this incising stage a drawing placed on top of color." Rather, this scratching-drawing in tones of blue constructed the form with color. In sections, clusters of scratches resemble atmospheric filmy washes. In between and on top of some of these tool marks Bittleman placed fine strokes of contrasting or adjacent colors (in pastel) which blend as one steps back to view the over-all color tapestry.

The painting was sprayed again, and then developed through several additional stages of (1) painting with Rhoplex and dry color, (2) pastels, and (3) incising with the sharp knife.

Reading the finished painting from the bottom up, at a distance of twelve feet, the viewer can trace the following color changes: dark Prussian blue, with rust-red flecks appearing underneath; above the blue, an orange band spotted with small yellows and blues; then gray covered with blue and vice versa — leading to the center of interest (upper center), vibrating yellows on top of blue. The dark in the upper right is primarily dull orange bleeding down to blue and yellow. The preceding is a general idea of the color movement in one direction.

In the central (yellow and blue) form, viewed from a distance of three feet, one can see the scratches which release the blue underneath; the pastel strokes on top of the knife marks can also be seen. The changes in color reading that take place as one walks toward a work of art from a great distance have

Detail, *Under The Wave.*

preoccupied Bittleman for some time. This concern has greatly influenced his work. During a recent trip to Europe he experienced a number of striking readings which he recounted in the course of the interview. At the Kroller-Muller Museum in Holland, a large Seurat, viewed from fifty feet, remained static. As he walked toward it, it began to "dance" and change radically — the optical mixtures of color were vividly separated into their components in several stages as he moved to within ten feet of the painting. Similarly, a small Van Gogh with a brilliant yellow-green sun was activated by small blue spots from the foreground as he came close. And at the Prado he observed a Bosch whose shapes unfolded: "The large shapes gradually dissolved as I moved nearer, dissolved into smaller shapes and then into independent forms within these shapes."

Such effects are repeated in Bittleman's pastels and particularly in *Under the Wave*. Optical mixtures of orange and blue (and yellow and blue) appear as one moves away. And new forms unfold as one advances — details which in themselves are vast panoramas. In short, one first sees large shapes and colors that change to vibrating colors and forms within the shapes; then, as one advances, the shapes reveal details which in themselves are miniature worlds. The complicated technique that Bittleman employs to produce these sensations — painting with brush, plastic, and pigment, then pastel, and then incising with a sharp instrument — works in the service of both his personal imagery and his spatial concepts.

Born in New York in 1933, ARNOLD BITTLEMAN *studied at the Rhode Island School of Design and Yale University School of Art and Architecture. He has had a one-man show at Kanegis Gallery and has also exhibited in group showings at the Museum of Modern Art, Whitney Museum, and the Pennsylvania Academy of Fine Arts. His works are included in collections of the Museum of Modern Art, Whitney Museum, Fogg Museum, Boston Museum of Fine Arts, Munson-Williams-Procter Institute, and Addison Gallery. He is represented by Kanegis Gallery in Boston and by Grace Borgenicht in New York.*

8.　　　　　　　　　　Gouache

Pat Adams

Large paintings, it seems, are the rule today. But "physically large" does not necessarily mean "visually large." For example, a photograph of a painting or a reproduction in a magazine usually does not indicate the size of the original. And reproductions of large paintings often appear visually small. But the opposite is true of Pat Adams' small gouaches — in reproduction they appear visually large. Her paintings create sustained yet expanding images despite the lack of obvious devices to establish gravity. This effect is achieved through a reciprocal action of shapes which alternately create tension and rest in a unified context. Her paintings are not merely a sum of equally weighted mosaic-like areas; instead the shapes seem dangerously perched and grouped in constantly surprising relationships. "Reading" her work one becomes aware of a constant movement, a change of focus, which is forced on the viewer. In short, her sense of constellation keeps her compositions from becoming, as she said when the author talked with her in her studio, "isolated and random phenomena."

Changing from a visual to a symbolic level, we should note that the elementary shapes which are part of the artist's constant vocabulary have been interpreted in many ways according to the viewer's frame of reference. Some relate her work to biology, others to astronomy. But although the essential shapes that inhabit her work have many different levels of meaning for both artist and viewer, the artist's primary concern is with composing "knots of isolated phenomena, sequences of edge and occurrence," into provocative yet ordered images.

A water-base medium, water color in particular, is usually associated with direct painting wherein the initial performance is also the final effect. Yet Pat Adams' work is often slowly and deliberately developed. Naturally the working process depends on the initial concept. In the artist's words: "Intuition always plays a role in composing — yet every rapid impulse is not worth saving. A moment of painting may be an experience for the artist, but it may not be transformed into art. It's not that I devalue directness," Miss Adams concluded, "but for me a sustained, all-connecting image is better than a captured moment." And before she explained her personal working methods and listed her tools and materials, she emphasized that the seemingly involved technique she now employs — which makes instant changes possible and which is elastic enough to allow for countless variations of development — was evolved because she "felt the need to be critical of the moment."

Miss Adams began the technical explanation by discussing the paper she employs. A smooth-surfaced paper, rather than a textured one, is preferred for two reasons: a textured paper competes with the combination of transparent and opaque effects the artist creates; secondly, a rough surface would prevent burnishing with a lintless cloth or a razor-like knife. "Burnishing periodically during the various stages brings out the color, unifies the surface, and produces a burr upon which further paint layers can attach themselves."

Pat Adams' paintings, for the most part, are developed in a series of alternating transparent and opaque layers. She constantly works on a group of paintings in different stages of development. Working loosely with transparent washes of watercolor or ink, she begins a number of paintings simultaneously. From this catalogue of rough ideas which these "starts" represent, she selects about one out of ten for further development. After the sketch is selected it may be thoroughly glazed with ink or watercolor and subsequently washed off and blotted. For the artist, these processes — washing out, staining, blotting — not only stimulate her vision but produce spatial decisions.

Pat Adams: *Quelle Heure Est-il?* Gouache. Collection M. J. Stewart.

The artist may employ sticks, sponges, and rags as well as brushes at the beginning and during the various stages: "Non-art instruments produce surprising and inspiring visual effects." A painting evolves as opaque colors are added with casein and tempera. The opaqued areas may be glazed again with watercolor and ink — and perhaps even washed out, blotted, and burnished. But a completed work never displays this overworking; the various processes operate in the service of visual development rather than technical virtuosity.

The materials employed are Winsor-Newton watercolors, Higgins and Pelikan colored inks, Shiva Nu-tempera, Le Franc gouache, and various makes of casein. Pro-White (Steig Products) is preferred to other whites because of its strong adhesive quality. It is employed "almost as a medium to resolve the incompatibility that sometimes occurs among the various water-soluble products such as ink and watercolor." Further, she finds that this white covers without becoming chalky — for chalkiness is a quality the artist prefers to avoid because it interferes with her desired imagery.

Pat Adams' concern with the constant interplay of shapes and interspace demanded the invention of a technique suited to constant change. Her very personal gouache technique, with its possibilities of change, with juxtaposition of opaque and transparent layers resulting from glazing, washing out, blotting and burnishing, offers the artist unlimited freedom in her search for an ever-expanding vision.

California-born (1928) PAT ADAMS *was educated at the University of California and studied in Florence, Italy, on a Fulbright scholarship. She has exhibited in one-man shows at the Zabriskie Gallery in New York and the Kanegis Gallery in Boston, and also participated in the Stable Gallery Annual and in a group show at the Whitney Museum. Her work was part of the Museum of Modern Art's "41 American Colorists" which was circulated in France. She is represented by the Zabriskie Gallery.*

9. Lucite Plastic with Oil

Gabor Peterdi

Synthetic resins are broadening the painter's media horizon, but some of the new plastics demand changes in ordinary working habits. Fortunately, the acrylic synthetic resins, of which Lucite is one, may be substituted for natural resins with ease; they are simple to prepare and to use with tube oil colors. Lucite was originally used by restorers and artists as a final varnish, and samples of it have been passing from painter to painter since 1950. It is as if painters had an underground through which information soon becomes common property.

Gabor Peterdi, who received a sample via this underground, has been using Lucite 44 since 1954. He was initially attracted to it because of its fast drying; it was easily adapted to his working methods and style; and he was able to achieve a consistent surface with it. His imagery, mostly horizontal and vertical forms that have disappearing edges, is punctuated with heavy, vivid color stabs. Since he wishes to show his tool marks on the canvas, Lucite serves his purpose, for it retains the brush stroke, whereas most oil-resin media tend to blur the stroke. Lucite will make a thinly applied brush stroke appear as an impasto.

Before he began to use Lucite, Mr. Peterdi used an equal mixture of dammar varnish, linseed oil, and turpentine. He then substituted Lucite for dammar and compared the results. Dammar, he noted, is more brittle and more easily damaged; a slight jolt on the back of the canvas readily produces cracks. Lucite is

flexible; it will "give" with the canvas. A recent experience is worth recounting here. Peterdi had completed a mural four feet by fourteen feet commissioned by the American President Lines. Soon after the work was dry it was rolled for shipment — a dangerous procedure for most oil paintings — but Peterdi was certain that the flexibility of the medium would prevent cracking.

Gabor Peterdi: *The Black Table,* 1956. Lucite Plastic with oil, 40 x 72".

He made these additional comparisons of Lucite with dammar. Lucite is never as glossy or glassy as dammar. Furthermore, Lucite appears to produce more light from the oil colors (test this by using alizarin or ultramarine with both media). Lastly, a Lucite medium is much faster drying, and yet dammar hardens rapidly after drying whereas Lucite hardens slowly.

The virtues of Lucite sound almost too good to be true. However, there are problems. If its solvent is too strong, Lucite can pick up the coat of paint underneath with the result that the undercoating may be softened. One has to be versatile to prevent it; one has to anticipate it in order to control it. Yet this supposed disadvantage has an advantage. Each coat merges with the coat underneath to form one over-all coat. The process of assimilation can be observed by this simple test. First, apply a number of coats of dammar on a piece of glass, waiting until each coat dries before the next application. Do the same with Lucite. Now scrape off each with a razor blade. You will notice that Lucite chips off in one coat. Obviously, Lucite has excellent adhesive properties. Nevertheless, it must be kept in mind that Lucite when mixed with a strong solvent tends to absorb the paint on lower surfaces.

One more problem confronts us: Lucite must be used with oil because most common solvents will destroy Lucite's film. The glue effect of oil will prevent this reaction. Mr. Peterdi uses at least thirty percent oil (Grumbacher) in his medium; he adds sun-thickened oil (Permanent Pigments) when he employs black to insure an even semigloss. (The jelly-like substance formed when Lucite is mixed with stand oil will thin with turpentine.)

In addition to Mr. Peterdi, Arthur Hoener (see page 37), a young artist, is also working with Lucite. He uses Lucite 45, which is slightly tougher but less flexible than Lucite 44. Mr. Hoener finds that a Lucite medium makes it possible to glaze with naturally opaque colors; the medium appears to make all colors transparent.

A word about Lucite itself: Lucite crystals are a white snow-like substance with a pleasant odor. They are best dissolved by two solvents: toluene, the most flexible of its family, and spirits of gum turpentine. Turpentine, used as the solvent, keeps the surface mat, but its use reduces one of Lucite's advantages, fast drying. Toluene, on the other hand, produces a fast-drying semigloss.

There follows the proportions for dissolving Lucite to achieve the same relative consistency as dammar: For an eight-pound cut use one ounce of Lucite by weight to one ounce of solvent by volume. To make an equivalent of a four-pound cut, simply double the proportion of solvent. Dupont claims stability to sunlight for Lucite. Additional technical information as well as a price list can be obtained by writing E. I. Dupont de Nemours and Co., Polychemicals Division, Wilmington, Delaware.*

As we have seen, Lucite has many remarkable features: it is flexible, never overshiny, it produces excellent light from oil colors, it dries rapidly. Moreover, it is easy to prepare, and reasonable in price. If used with the right solvent Lucite will not affect the paint underneath, and although it requires mixing with oil, it yellows no more than an ordinary oil-resin medium.

———

*Also available at Almac Plastics, Inc., 600 Broadway, New York 12, N.Y.

———

GABOR PETERDI, *who came to this country from Hungary where he was born in 1915, studied in Budapest, Rome, and Paris. He now teaches at Hunter College and the Yale University School of Art and Architecture. Widely exhibited in group shows in the United States and Europe, he has had one-man shows in various parts of the world: Budapest, Czechoslovakia, Rome, the Jean Bucher gallery in Paris, Smithsonian Institute (Washington, D.C.), Kanegis Gallery (Boston), Schermerhorn Gallery (Beloit, Wis.), Brooklyn Museum, and the following New York galleries: Norlyst, Laurel, Julian Levy, and Grace Borgenicht. His works have also been widely collected: Sao Paulo Museum (Brazil,) Kunst Pa (Norway), the Museums of Budapest, Prague, and Rome, Museum of Modern Art, Metropolitan and Brooklyn Museums, New York Public Library, Chicago Art Institute, and 35 other museums and collections. Mr. Peterdi has won a Ford Foundation grant for 1960, among other awards, including one from the Brooklyn and the Associated American Artists Graphic Prize. He is represented by the Grace Borgenicht gallery in N. Y., the Kanegis Gallery in Boston, and the Schermerhorn Gallery in Beloit, Wisconsin.*

Esther Geller: *Paradise Screen*, 1952. Encaustic.

10.   Encaustic

Esther Geller

Wax painting, practiced many years ago by the Egyptians, Greeks, and Romans, is sometimes called encaustic — a word that literally means "burned in" and therefore implies the use of heat. As practiced today, the process involves the heating and mixing together of dry pigment and wax, with a portable heating instrument being employed to burn in the mixture. It may be asked why this technique has been revived in the modern period and adopted to contemporary modes of expression. Possibly, it is because of the special optical qualities with which the wax is endowed: its translucence and its brilliance. Such at least are the features which have attracted Esther Geller, who after studying with Karl Zerbe, the painter largely responsible for reviving encaustic, has been experimenting since 1940 with encaustic medium. In the course of her work, she has developed a number of methods which are of general interest to painters.

Miss Geller employs a two-burner electric plate with rheostat heat control. The palette is an ungalvanized steel box (it should be noted that galvanized steel discolors pigment). This box, which has large holes cut out over the heating units, is placed on top of the electric stove. Circulating air keeps the heat even. The wax is heated on the palette, mixed with dry pigment, and applied to board or canvas, where it dries immediately. The "burning in" can be done during the process of painting or at its conclusion. The preferred instrument is a tungsten unit plugged into an asbestos-covered handle. Miss Geller prefers this instrument to a heat lamp or blow torch; it is light in weight and gives enough heat to fuse the pigment-and-wax-mixture thoroughly, so as to insure adhesion and hardening of the surface.

Now let us proceed to the preparation of the wax medium. Experimentation and research led Miss Geller to choose beeswax, which she found to be the most transparent of the waxes. She prefers bleached or white beeswax to the yellow virgin beeswax, for the yellow wax discolors the blues. She also discovered that virgin wax contains pollen, which may affect anyone with a slight allergy. Therefore, although virgin wax, with its honey fragrance, is pleasant to work with, Miss Geller considers bleached wax distinctly more practical. She recommends the purchase of the material stamped "pure beeswax," available at most art shops or drugstores.

The bleached wax is added to dammar crystals which have been melted in a can on the stove palette. Miss Geller's formula is one part dammar crystals to two parts wax, and since she uses a rigid support (gesso on Masonite), no oil need be added. However, she advises an addition of 10% linseed oil to this mixture if one should need a more pliable medium to paint on canvas. The medium is cut into cakes when cool.

When one is ready to paint, a cake is remelted and dry pigment added. The new mixture is now ready to be applied to the support with palette knives or brushes. It should be noted that prolonged contact with the hot plate will scorch a bristle brush, which therefore must be used with care. For glazing, sable brushes are recommended. It is true that turpentine can be used to thin the glaze mixture, but Miss Geller prefers to dispense with it. (Of course, she uses turpentine to clean her brushes.) "Burning in" completes the process.

Miss Geller's answers to specific questions filled in a number of details. When asked if a certain proportion of wax and dammar to pigment is required to insure permanency, she replied that "any proportion is feasible so long as it holds on to the

Esther Geller "burning in" an encaustic painting.

support." Miss Geller further informed me that she has not encountered any fading or cracking of surface in her long experience. But the proportion of wax and dammar to pigment, she explained, does influence the surface; a lot of pigment and little medium produce a mat surface, whereas a greater proportion of wax makes it possible to polish the painting at the end. Moreover, a great deal of dammar makes for a glossier surface. She pointed out that through his formula the painter can dictate the kind of surface he desires. Even thickening agents such as powdered clay and lithopone can be used to heighten the impasto.

Or if a polished-gold effect is desired, Miss Geller recommends placing gold leaf on the gesso in the traditional glue and clay-bole method; a high gloss can thereby be achieved through burnishing. On the other hand, one can produce a dull gold by applying Polymer Tempera to the chosen area and applying leaf while the Polymer is wet. In general, leaf is applied first to whatever areas the painter desires.

Does the use of heating apparatus make for size limitation? "I myself find it possible to work in any size," Miss Geller replied. "The principal limitation is adjusting to a different tempo of painting. Encaustic has a tempo of its own." By this she means that although the hot wax dries immediately on touching the canvas, the pausing to "burn in" sections of the painting does interrupt normal oil-painting working methods. Wax does not blend; blending of edges, when desired, is achieved in the fusing process. A great deal of heating softens boundaries, causing them to melt — blurring the hard edge. The burning-in process, therefore, is not just a mechanical procedure, but rather part of the actual painting process.

The encaustic method thus requires not only special equipment, but a period of apprenticeship. Yet, if one admires the color brilliancy and the translucent quality of wax, the immediate drying and the challenge of an adjusted tempo, the time invested will not seem a major obstacle.

Note: For an extended account of the process the reader is referred to *Encaustic: Materials and Methods*, by Francis Pratt and Becca Fizell (Lear Publishers, New York, 1949)

ESTHER GELLER *was born in 1921 in Boston, where she studied with Karl Zerbe at the School of the Boston Museum of Fine Arts. Presently living and teaching in Natick, Mass., Miss Geller has exhibited in one-man shows at the Boris Mirski Gallery, which represents her, and at the Addison Gallery. Her paintings are in collections of the Boston Museum and the Addison Gallery.*

11.   Weaving as Pictorial Art

Anni Albers

Tapestries in general employ an ancient method of weaving, the weft used as sole agent, covering the warp threads completely and resulting in an even surface. It is a technique that has been and is being used for textile pictures, based on painters cartoons — a transposition of pictures composed by other means into the textile medium. By contrast, a tapestry produced by Anni Albers denotes a method in which the threads and their interlacing are used as the elements of composition. In short, her pictorial weavings are developed in terms of the material. The invention and execution of these tapestries, then, is close to the *process* of painting a picture and is not the indirect method of using a painting as a pictorial basis. Invention and intuition, as in all artistic efforts, play their part in this work at the loom and in what the artist here calls "listening" to the possibilities of the medium. And as Mrs. Albers detailed her method and ideas in her interview, the parallel to the act of painting became more obvious.

But first let us go back to discuss weaving in general and Anni Albers' views in particular: "Hand-weaving today deals mostly with decorative fabrics. What I am trying to do is to keep fabrics intended for practical use as useful as possible. I try not to obscure their usefulness by emphasizing decorative elements, that is, I try to keep them as anonymous as possible. My concern with formal elements of composition comes out in concentrated form in my woven pictures, which are useless, of course, in any practical sense." In her useful textiles, designed to be produced on machine looms, Mrs. Albers has experimented with a number of newly developed fibers, among them fiberglas. When she emphasizes the *anonymous* aspects of her useful fabrics, she also implies

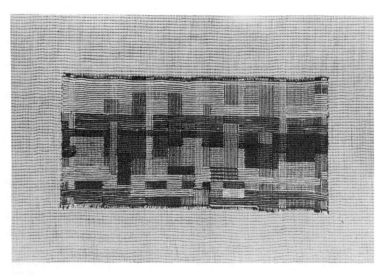

Anni Albers: *City*, 1949. Weaving, 17½ x 26½".

a desire for a *timeless* one, as opposed to an interest in the latest fashion which invariably is soon replaced by another fashion. This phase of her work is mainly related to an architectural environment. And in this context she quoted Paul Klee discussing some weaving done at the Bauhaus: "After all, textiles are serving objects." And Mrs. Albers added, "He meant to give us a warning not to make fabrics that are too independent, but to make fabrics that assume their proper place in the surroundings."

Still another role in Anni Albers' career is that of teaching. For sixteen years she was assistant professor of art at Black Mountain College and taught weaving there. She gave seminars at the Museum of Modern Art, the Philadelphia Museum School, the University of Hawaii, the Minneapolis School of Art, etc., and lectured at a number of Museums and Universities. Her teaching has not dealt primarily with technology, but rather, its interworking with formal, visual problems and with philosophical aspects.

Now let us return to our main concern here, the pictorial

weavings which are not conceived as "useful" or "anonymous" or necessarily as part of an architectural setting. Instead they are conceived in terms of formal, visual art. The weaving of these tapestries begins, we learned, with the choice of threads of different character in regard to color, twist, lustre, weight, etc., that is, with the choice of the palette, so to speak. The work grows out of the visual results of the intersecting threads on the loom, that is, out of the interplay of color and structure producing shapes and interspaces in the given framework. The thread becomes roughly the equivalent of a paint stroke. And the manipulation of the threads produces overlaps which are the result of varying densities in the basically vertical and horizontal scheme of interpenetration throughout the weaver's pictorial plane. For example in "City" (herewith reproduced) made of linen and cotton threads in black, white, and neutral colors, the differences in emphasis on either the horizontal or vertical interlacings give some areas the illusion of transparency, as do also the differences in thickness of threads and their groupings. It follows, that this interaction of color, structure, texture, density, openness, etc. must be composed in response to the formative demand of all weaving, the interlacing in both the horizontal and vertical direction. This interplay used by Anni Albers permits both warp, the vertical element, and weft, the horizontal one, to be active, in distinction to the established tapestry technique which, as mentioned before, leaves all compositional variations to the weft which alone is visible on the surface.

Although this manner of composing with the interplay of forms resembles painting, the work of the weaver is made difficult in one respect, the problem of judging the work in progress while on the loom. The weaver must, of necessity, construct his work much like a building, area upon area, while he is planning the total effect. He cannot correct parts, nor can he overlook the whole, as a painter can, when he steps back from the easel to make a critical estimation. (That weaving also is a slow procedure plays its part in increasing the difficulties of work). Needless to add, the limitations of the medium dictate the range of possibilities and call for great inventiveness.

In connection with the limitations of a technique, Anni Albers emphasizes that the author should be a listener to technique and medium, that is, he should be open to suggestion coming from *this side*. Such passiveness, she believes, releases intuition and imagination and will lead one better than when one makes a conscious effort to be leading oneself. If those concerned with the making of art today would experiment more with a resistant than with an obedient medium, there would be less need to turn to introspection as the main catalyst. Ultrasubjectiveness, she believes, can hardly be our salvation.

To sum up — Anni Albers' work in weaving, which transforms her material, various strands of colored threads, into a formal visual experience, resembles painting in many ways: the choice of the palette, the structure, the texture, and the invented surface tension within the formal concept, all being used to construct a spatial environment in terms of the medium. It is a medium which demands a high level of organization for the artist to form an ordered pictorial vision since he is unable to view the entire work in progress. She employs what is generally not considered a medium of so-called fine art, but a craft medium, to produce pictorial art.

Born in Berlin, ANNI ALBERS *studied in her native Germany at the School of Applied Arts in Hamburg and at the Bauhaus in Weimar and in Dessau. She has taught at the now defunct Black Mountain College and lectured at the Philadelphia Museum School, University of Hawaii, San Francisco Museum, Minnesota School of Art, Brooklyn Museum, Syracuse University, and Carnegie Institute of Technology. Mrs. Albers has had one-man shows at the Museum of Modern Art (circulating exhibit), Wadsworth Atheneum (Hartford), Currier Gallery of Art (Manchester, N.H.), Honolulu Academy of Art, and Massachusetts Institute of Technology. Her works are included in collections of the Museum of Modern Art, Busch-Reisinger Museum (Harvard University), Museum of Cranbrook Academy of Art (Mich.), Cooper Union Museum, Brooklyn Museum, and Currier Gallery of Art (N.H.).*

12.   Paper Collage

Irwin Rubin

Today, a painter working with collage can find little information which will aid him in choosing permanent materials. As a result, an artist involved with a newer visual mode, and with permanency, must do independent research. Irwin Rubin, who has been working with collage (in his case, paper collage) for five years, is one of the few who have made a careful investigation of their materials. The information he has accumulated should prove of value for the many painters who now are working with collage.

Rubin believes that the early collages by Braque and Picasso were obviously well constructed for they are still in "good health." By contrast, the Dada-inspired collages, for which permanency admittedly was not considered important, range in physical condition from almost complete disintegration to an all-over "patina of time" (to quote a recent collage exhibition catalogue). It was a fear of this patina which prompted Mr. Rubin's research. He investigated the composition of paper, the processes of its manufacture, the cause of its deterioration. He tested colored papers, and he also experimented with coating and gluing. In an interview with the author he recommended specifications for permanent paper which are reported below.

At the outset, Rubin explained that paper for collage has to withstand aging rather than handling, because it is only in the construction stage that handling may be excessive. To illustrate

Irwin Rubin: untitled paper collage.

deterioration, he exhibited pages from two newspapers. One was in seemingly perfect condition — *Harper's Weekly*, dated February 4, 1860. By contrast the *New York Times* of October 26, 1954 was stained a pale burnt sienna. To explain the contrast Mr. Rubin listed some causes of deterioration: chemical residues from manufacturing, certain fungi (which cause foxing), addition of mineral matter, and the greatest menace of all, over-acidity, which may be caused by faulty removal of residue in the bleaching process.

We returned to the two newspapers. *Harper's Weekly* was printed on a rag paper; the *New York Times,* on mechanical wood paper. Rag paper, made from cotton and flax, contains the greatest percentage of pure cellulose—one key to permanency. Paper-making materials in order of the amount of cellulose were listed as follows by Mr. Rubin: cotton, flax, mulberry, hemp, esparto, straw, and mechanical wood. "Yet," Mr. Rubin added, "more than the initial choice of the fibers themselves, the process of its manufacture will ultimately decide the permanence of the paper. Even mechanical wood — if properly processed — can produce a durable paper. Whatever material may be used for making paper, certain procedures are generally followed: reducing to fibrous state, bleaching, beating to a pulp with water, and lastly, converting the pulp into paper."

At this point we discussed the relative merits of handmade versus machine-made paper. Mr. Rubin explained that the above procedures are the same except that handmade paper is produced sheet by sheet instead of on a continuous web of woven wire. Handmade paper was recommended because it is less likely to have harmful additives and is constructed with equal stress in both horizontal and vertical directions. To distinguish handmade from machine-made paper Mr. Rubin suggested that one tear the paper in question from all sides rapidly. If it resists more on one side than the other it is machine-made. Or, if wet and pressed between blotting paper, machine-made paper will spread most in one direction. To sum up, Mr. Rubin gave six specifications for the best paper: (1) handmade; (2) 100% rag — new linen, cotton, flax or hemp — undyed and unbleached; (3) no added filler or color; (4) free from starch, rosin, or any added mineral matter; (5) size should be animal gelatin; (6) relatively acid-free. "These criteria may seem extreme," Mr. Rubin stated, "but a collage is only as permanent as its most perishable paper. And weaknesses in paper are often communicable."

We turned next to the testing of colored paper for light fastness. Mr. Rubin had collected as many types of colored paper as possible and cut a three-inch square from each. A one-inch square of black photographic paper was placed in the center to protect this area from light. After exposing all the samples to direct sunlight for two weeks and comparing the exposed and protected areas, he felt he had an indication of the degree to which one colored paper will fade in relation to others. The colored paper which best withstood the sunlight were Color Aid and Color Vue papers. But even these in their brightest colors showed signs of fading. These tests prompted Mr. Rubin to make his own colored paper.

Oil paint can be used to color paper so long as the paper is sized with gelatin on both sides. Turpentine, however, was found to contain acids which tended to damage the paper, and therefore Mr. Rubin abandoned oil in favor of water-base media. For pasting papers coated with casein and other water-thinned media, he employed flour, dextrin, and gelatin. The expense of coating vast amounts of paper with durable tube colors prompted him, in turn, to search for an adhesive which could be also used as a coating vehicle (with dry pigments), a medium which could be used for both coating and gluing and would also save time (and perhaps would be sounder technically). Such an adhesive would have to meet many requirements. It should neither discolor nor be subject to mold. It should produce a strong bond and give maximum ease of preparation and handling. Further, it should be fast-drying and have a reasonably low acid content. A medium or glue which meets these requirements is polyvinyl acetate emulsified. Of all the commercial preparations of this material, Mr. Rubin found that Polymer Tempera (see page 31) dried clearest and had a controlled acid content. He has been using it for three years. But his search is continuing; at present he is experimenting with other plastics and with plastic paper.

"These experiments may seem an overconcern with permanence," Mr. Rubin concluded, "but collage for me is not a medium to prepare studies to be carried out in another medium. At present it is my major medium. In order to give it meaning, this search was necessary."

IRWIN RUBIN *was born in Brooklyn in 1930 and studied at the Brooklyn Museum Art School, Cooper Union, and Yale University School of Art and Architecture. Now painting in New York, he formerly taught at Florida State University and at the University of Texas. Mr. Rubin is represented by Bertha Schaefer Gallery in New York.*

13.   Collage and Painting

Conrad Marca-Relli

Conrad Marca-Relli began to work in collage in 1952. His work in this idiom was the subject of an interview with the author in which he discussed his materials, his working methods, and his attitudes. First, he emphasized that "I have been working in collage as a result of genuine need; a medium is adopted by an artist to express himself more clearly in a particular way." And he added, "Collage for me is not study, diversion, or experiment. Instead, it has become my painting form." Yet, Marca-Relli felt that, like all media, collage can easily be abused. He agreed that if the manner becomes more important than the matter or image or formal relations, that is, if we see the pasted materials (the "what") before we see the interaction of shape, line, color, etc. (the "how"), then the medium remains solely a method. In short, the materials must add up to an "image" which transforms the material.

Marca-Relli's initial use of collage was a logical development of several white-on-white paintings. And his painting prior to collage also contained large flat shapes — shapes in an interior space and landscapes with dense black skies stretching over block-like buildings. The step from painting to collage, then, did not force a radical change in his formal language. The earliest works with collage, modest in dimension, were in the service of adding a vocabulary of interlocking and overlapping shapes. In addition, lines were produced by the edges of the shapes; the back of each

cut-out shape was coated with a dark color which stained the edges. These edges created a network of alternately continuous and broken line which defined the shapes and stressed the tensions of the overlaps. In a subsequent series of white-on-white pasted canvases, he produced what appeared to be, from a distance, delicate line drawings.

Marca-Relli's emphasis on the line and the interlocking shape has explained the possibilities of the medium. Yet critics have, at times, related his work to texture study. Perhaps because Braque's collages were somewhat textural in nature, all collage is automatically linked to texture. "I do not create space through changes of texture," Marca-Relli commented. "My concern has

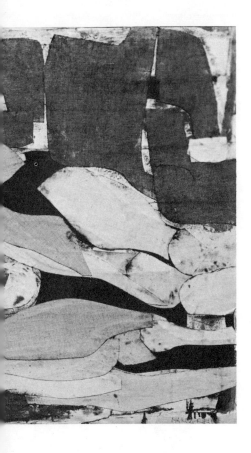

Conrad Marca-Relli:
M-4-56. Collage, 25 x 45"

been more with color than texture. The texture produced is the consequence of the pasting as form — the working method." His first collages were produced with primed (white) and unprimed canvas. The interaction of these two whites produced a play of transparency and opaqueness. True, he purposely limited himself at first to whites, but he gradually added natural-colored tan linens; it was the play of a limited color range rather than texture which led him to expand his palette. In his more recent work he has, in his own words, "felt the urge to use a wider color range." He therefore employs paint in combination with collage — large broad areas of reds, blues, and mustard yellow. For Marca-Relli this is "a natural growth of my color interest."

Conrad Marca-Relli: *Pamplona,* 1958. Collage and paint 4′9″ x 6′5″.

There are some misconceptions about Marca-Relli's method of cutting shapes. "I do not pre-cut shapes to fit a predetermined arrangement. I never measure the area to be worked." The table on which he cuts out the shapes, he explained, is about ten feet away from the painting. His only preparations are drawings (rehearsals) which "build up the rhythm of the type of interlocking to be employed." Marca-Relli works directly, that is, "spontaneously," but he does not depend solely on accident or the "emotional moment." Yet he wants to preserve the "freshness" of Expressionism, and he feels that collage gives him a method of working simultaneously on many levels: he is free to change the form relationships immediately. He can blot out darks with a fresh white surface, paint and cover over and over again, correcting the relations as he sees fit until he reaches what he considers a "permanent clarity." "But this method," he emphasized, "has its pitfalls. Fear of making changes — of destroying relationships too fast (in fact, in seconds) — makes this a difficult medium." Coupling immediate action with a desire for a permanent clarity seems to combine two antagonistic concepts. But the power to destroy or construct in an instant is inherent in the medium. Marca-Relli summed it up this way: "I want to be able to do it over and over again until the action is satisfactory to me. I know when it clicks, and I want to be free — not to depend on accident, but to solve finally and with immediacy."

At this point Marca-Relli commented on the changes in his work over the past seven years. At first he constructed single figures. Gradually he began to work with groups of figure in what he calls "the architecture of an event." (see *The Battle* at the Metropolitan Museum). At present the shapes he employs are, for him, the synthesis: "The forces themselves are my concern. Yet the same abstract forces were present when the figure was the basis." And he added, "I never used the figure naturalistically; it was always distorted to fit a role in the painting."

Finally, he listed the glues he has employed for pasting. He began by using roofing tar, and he has employed oil paint — especially lead white, which has a strong glue action. He has also employed heated-wax-in-turpentine mix combined with dammar varnish. At present he employs plastic glues — polyvinyl acetate emulsified, such as Soho, Elmer's, or the Italian equivalent, Vinavil. He prefers the plastics because they minimize shrinkage.

To sum up, Marca-Relli has employed collage to combine an expressionistic attitude of direct attack and immediate change with the classical concept of a perfected spatial environment. He does not employ collage as a sum of textures; rather, his interest has been in a limited range of color which he has recently expanded to allow for primary colors to play against the black, white, and tans of the canvas. The color has been added at times by painting, at times by colored material. His use of the darkened edge assumes a contrapuntal role to what he considers the essence of his use of collage, the interlocking of open and closed forms. And let us note that he has changed the scale of collage; his fluid technique of pasting and painting permits him to work on wallsized paintings with ease. In his words: "There are no limitations to any medium. My problem has been to use collage in what I feel is a natural way."

CONRAD MARCA-RELLI *was born in Winthrop, Mass. in 1913 and studied in New York. He has been visiting critic at Yale University School of Art and Architecture and visiting professor at the University of California at Berkeley. Recipient of an award from the Ford Foundation and a major prize from the Art Institute of Chicago, Mr. Marca-Relli has exhibited in one-man shows at the Stable Gallery (New York), Frank Perls Gallery (Hollywood), Galleria La Tartaruga (Rome), Galleria Naviglio (Milan), and the Kootz Gallery (New York), who represent him. He has also participated in group shows here and abroad. Collections including his works are in the Metropolitan Museum, Museum of Modern Art, Art Institute of Chicago, Guggenheim Museum, Carnegie Institue of Technology, Minneapolis Institute of Art, Albright Galleries (Buffalo), Detroit Institute of Art, Whitney Museum, and Washington University (St. Louis).*

14.   Space and Expression

James Brooks

James Brooks: *Boon*. Oil. Collection Tate Gallery, London.

To discuss materials and related methods with a painter without probing his aesthetic and "compositional" attitudes is to draw what we feel to be a false line between craft and vision. Therefore in our interview with James Brooks we discussed a wide range of topics: space and expression, nature and art, decoration in painting. But we did begin with materials.

Paint for some artists — Brooks among them — is a sensuous material. Mr. Brooks feels that the inherent nature of paint is an important aspect of the painter's equipment. He therefore employs interacting areas of transparent, translucent, and opaque pigments which are produced without forcing texture. This interplay of surface effects, which Brooks merely calls "letting the paint act naturally," is put to the service of spatial activity; it is a part — even if a small part — of the "expression" in a Brooks painting. In *Boon,* here reproduced, the blacks, which appear opaque in the photograph, are in reality translucent; one can see through the blacks to the light which is below the surface. It should be noted that this use of pigment to produce light and texture is not an altogether prevalent attitude. Some painters feel that the material, paint, is something that naturally resists personal image-making; they purposely fail to take advantage of the possibilities inherent in this flexible medium by disregarding its surface qualities.

Brooks has constantly experimented with media. He has employed enamels on Bemis' Osnaburg cloth and on cotton duck canvas. Polyvinyl acetate and Rhoplex (pages 31 & 37) have also been used in his experiments during the past few years. At present he employs Lucite (see page 55), a plastic which he dissolves in turpentine and to which he adds about 10% linseed oil. This mixture produces a fairly non-reflective surface — which he prefers. Cans of Behlen's paste-form pigments in linseed oil are employed with the medium. He thins the paint with an extender (asbestine) when he wants a color that has both viscosity and transparency. Brooks prefers this ready-to-use canned paint for his many large-scale works, but he also employs tube colors when particular hues are wanted. His enjoyment of "physical involvement which a large area demands of a painter" dates from the execution of murals during the days of the Federal Art Project. (The mural in the Marine Building at La Guardia Airport in New York City is one of his works dating from that period.)

At this point in the discussion we branched out into the topic of "self-expression," a term which Brooks considers to be much-abused. He thinks that every brush stroke placed on canvas, gentle or violent, of necessity is self-expression. More important: "A painting is expressive of everything the artist identifies himself with." And for James Brooks expression in the use of space produced by changing formal relationships "is the painter's method." This interaction of shape and color — that is, the groupings or relationships they may produce — "transmits an impulse which is the image and meaning of a painting."

Mr. Brooks assured the author that his paintings, filled with baroque rhythms which suggest natural growth (as opposed to man-made straight lines), do not represent either a "return to nature" or, as some painters may call it, "a going forward to nature," because for him "painting is part of nature." His belief in this concept led him to decline participation in the "Nature in Abstraction" exhibition at the Whitney Museum in 1958.

Next we discussed "painting and decoration." Brooks disagreed with the definition that a painting — as opposed to decoration — possesses focal points and has a beginning and an end. Instead he feels the difference lies between "pleasure and exhilaration" on the one hand, and the "frightening" and the "unknown" on the other. "Both qualities are present in the best paintings. If a painting is all pleasurable," he continued, "it is decorative. On the other hand, when the unknown enters, one receptive to painting may be possessed by the presented image in a physical way — one's hair may stand on end."

Brooks also commented on the view that it is necessary, or at least helpful, to know the painter to understand his work properly. He believes this is a false concept because it is the painting which presents the artist's vision — the painting which is the carrier of the artist's ultimate biography. "Facts about the artist's life may be interesting," Brooks added, "but only in a peripheral sense. It is the painting that I prefer to know." By way of illustration Brooks pointed out that the painters he now admires most, Piero and Giotto, possess a monolithic quality completely unlike anything in his own work. This fact may be interesting to a viewer looking at a Brooks painting, but he does not see how it can help anyone to participate in the painting.

Later, we inquired about the titles which Mr. Brooks gives his paintings. This topic perhaps also turned out to be peripheral, since with Mr. Brooks, it is simply a housekeeping problem rather than one relating directly to the visual. Brooks titles his paintings primarily for identification. About ten years ago he began to employ numbers and letters to indicate the order in which they were completed in a particular year. He soon found, however, that this system was unsatisfactory. He therefore puts together syllable combinations which he can remember: *Altoon, Floxurn, Holdan.* He has also used the names of towns in Texas which he knew in his youth: Falfurias, Quero.

Finally, Brooks commented on a universal problem of the artist — how to confront painting and life freshly each day. The ideal combination, in his view, is to be able to weld a child's awareness on one's own collected, complicated adult experience.

Born in St. Louis in 1906, JAMES BROOKS *studied with Nicolaides and Robertson at the Art Students League, and with Wallace Harrison. He has taught at Pratt Institute and has been a visiting critic at Yale University School of Art and Architecture. Mr. Brooks has had several New York one-man shows, at Peridot Gallery, Grace Borgenicht Gallery, and Stable Gallery. He was one of the Museum of Modern Art's "12 Americans" in 1956 and has also been exhibited in group shows throughout the United States and Europe. Collections which include his works are the Whitney Museum, Metropolitan Museum, Museum of Modern Art, Brooklyn Museum, Albright Art Gallery (Buffalo), Guggenheim Museum, Wadsworth Athenaeum (Hartford), and Tate Gallery (London). Agent for Mr. Brooks is the Kootz Gallery in New York.*

15.   Color Is Magic

Josef Albers

"I am neither an abstractionist nor an expressionist painter —
my primary concern is the interaction of color." So began Josef
Albers in an interview with the author. Albers, a veteran of
hundreds of exhibitions the world over and a leader in art edu-
cation, is also a cogent writer on art. In the interview he discussed both color and his personal technique.

Let us continue with his view on color by quoting a catalogue of 1952: ". . . a knowing colorist can make equal colors
look different and different colors alike; thus bright looks pale
and dull intensive. He turns warm into cool and the opposite;
exchanges advancing and receding properties at liberty; makes
opaque look transparent; definite shapes unrecognizable. In
short, he not only recognizes that color is deceiving us all the
time, but uses color as an acting agent, changing its identity in
many ways." Mr. Albers detailed these remarks by pointing out
that adjacent colors exert a change on their neighbors. A stronger
color pushes the neighboring color towards its opposite (com-
plementary). A light color makes its neighboring color look
darker, and vice versa. Secondly, the larger color area influences
the neighboring color in the same way as does pronunciation of
shape. And thirdly, the placement above or below, to the left or

Josef Albers: *Homage to the Square.* Oil.

right (constellation), and whether the boundaries are firm or loose change the appearance of colors.

These ideas, for Albers, are not simply a theory but rather a working thesis which he practices from day to day in his paintings. Nor are his paintings merely *information* or *investigation*. Critics have likened them to icons in their light-giving quality — for color here is the "light source" (as opposed to paintings where light is created by the contrast between light and dark). And although Albers may be considered a geometric painter, his interest in geometry is again secondary to color interaction. Geometric subdivisions in his series "Homage to the Square," for example, may remain constant, but color appears to change the squares in size and distance. The same-size squares, when viewed in sequence, seem either to shrink or expand — or on occasion to blend with their adjacent squares. In short, "acting color" makes shapes as well as colors lose their identity. Albers' concern, then, "with the illusion that color is deceiving us all the time" is employed to produce new psychological effects with an economy of means. A much-published statement reveals his credo:

The origin of art:

The discrepancy between physical fact and psychic effect

The content of art:.

Visual formulation of our reaction to life

The measure of art:

The ratio of effort to effect

The aim of art:

Revelation and evocation of vision

The second half of our interview concerned Albers' methods of painting. He began by discussing supports and grounds for oil painting. Masonite ($\frac{1}{8}$ inch, untempered), is preferred for three reasons: "Masonite has wall character. Canvas has little resistance. Canvas stretchers, having only full-inch lengths, limit proportion." The desire to have his colors as brilliant as possible has led him to constant experimentation with grounds. A semi-absorbent white casein ground which "keeps the pigment on top and not the oil" initially attracted him. But this ground dulled the deep earth colors so much that he had to apply varnish to judge color relationships. Moreover, he found it impossible to repair simple scratches — it was impossible to match the tone created by the gradual sinking in of the colors. He therefore abandoned casein and experimented with a ground which is non-absorbent, alkyd (resin) enamel. Alkyd enamel presented opposing problems; this ground is so resistant that drying time is greatly prolonged. And colors that take a lot of oil in grinding — such as ivory black — produced a very slick surface. Albers countered the excess oil by adding pure calcium carbonate (whiting), which does not affect the color, to the black. And he even dried out these oiliest of colors on a blotter prior to use. At present he is experimenting with a more flexible semi-absorbent ground of Rhoplex acrylic emulsion produced by Permanent Pigments (Liquitex). His first experiments with this ground have yielded color with "full brilliance." A pure-white ground displays every color to its full intensity; as the oil film becomes thinner on aging, it reflects the white undercoat, adding to the luminosity. Albers adopted the white ground when he was a student of Max Doerner in Germany.

Albers avoids mixing colors as much as possible. He believes that any mixing reduces color or light intensity, often both. Only in mixing blues and pinks does he add white to his colors. To protect himself from mixing and to have a real choice of color, he has acquired a large collection of tube paints. As colors of the same names from different manufacturers vary, he has, for example, up to six different shades of cadmium yellow medium. He paints in one primary coat, applying the color with a palette knife. Needless to add, he avoids all painting media, for he feels too much oil changes the color. Texture is accepted only when unavoidable with transparent or semi-transparent pigments — not for additional surface effects nor for "personal handwriting."

Albers' paintings are varnished when they are thoroughly dry. The smaller paintings are varnished with a brush with either dammar varnish or "M" varnish (Robinson). The larger paintings are sprayed with polyvinyl acetate or Lucite 45, thinned with xylene. The final varnish, he feels, is necessary as a protection for an oil film.

Finally at the end of the interview, Albers made the following comment about the relationship between color and the source of light.

"There is an old rule for painters that landscape paintings begun outdoors should be finished indoors, because it is there that they will be shown.

"This conclusion is a consequence of the difference between outdoor light and indoor light, and this difference influences color relationships considerably. But also indoor light changes a great deal throughout the day. For the most part, indoor light is warmer than outdoor light, but towards evening it is cooler than outdoor light which in darkening also turns much warmer.

"Thus sensitive eyes will notice that in daytime the reds in a painting dominate, and that in twilight the blues become more active. Still more changes in light occur later in the evening with artificial light. Furthermore, we must be aware that paintings are seen by far more people in artificial light than in natural light. This is something of a rule, particularly now when more and more galleries and museums prefer cold and warm artificial light to constantly changing natural light.

"As a consequence, I myself prefer to paint under artificial light. I use mostly fluorescent light — just as in good galleries, a combination of warm with cool. I also can switch easily to incandescent light which is extremely warm and therefore permits better comparing of warm colors.

"Anyway, I see no reason for the painter to depend on daylight which changes continually — changes in two directions: in its light intensity and in its color intensity. The very famous north-light for ateliers, though it provides reflected light and protection from direct sunlight, seems not only superfluous, but unnatural and more artificial than all truly artificial light."

To sum up: Albers' work with interacting color has produced a simple, direct oil-painting technique ("The measure of art: the ratio of effort to effect") in which a constantly changing instrumentation varies his palette from painting to painting. One final note: Recently Professor Albers retired after thirty-five years of teaching (Bauhaus, Black Mountain, and Yale) to devote full time to painting. At seventy he possesses a sense of mission rarely encountered in "younger" painters.

German-born JOSEF ALBERS *was a student at the Bauhaus in Weimar where he also taught, later transferring to Desau when the school was removed there. In addition he has taught in Berlin and, since coming to America, at Black Mountain College (now discontinued), Cincinnati Art Academy, Pratt Institute, and Harvard Summer School. More recently, he was Professor of Art at Yale University School of Arts and Architecture and Chairman of the Department of Art (1951-58). He has also lectured in Cuba, Mexico, Chile, Peru, Hawaii, and Germany. His works have been exhibited in the leading galleries and museums in the United States and Europe. Mr. Albers is represented by two New York galleries, Sidney Janis and The Contemporaries, of which the latter handles his prints.*

16.   The Permanent Palette

Leonard Bocour

The sight of buckets of cadmiums, cobalts, and earth colors being mixed and tubed is an exciting experience for a painter. But Leonard Bocour's one-floor factory loft near Tenth Avenue in New York has an added interest: as one steps off the elevator into two adjacent offices, one becomes aware of many paintings on the walls, from floor to ceiling, and many more stacked against the walls. These works represent twenty-seven years of collecting paintings. Leonard Bocour, originally trained as a painter, first became interested in the materials of painting when he met Emil Ganso. Ganso, who owned a Doerner book in the original German edition, made Leonard Bocour aware of the "rich lore of craft." "Of course," as Mr. Bocour remarked to the author, "since the thirties, with the appearance of Doerner in English and with the publication of Ralph Mayer's book, painters can acquire adequate technical knowledge. In the early thirties I began preparing my own paints. Before long I was making paints for friends. The next step found me in business." The following expert information on the permanent palette and some problems of manufacturing artists' oil colors is based on a discussion the author had with Mr. Bocour in his office.

Permanent white pigments were discussed first. Lead white (or flake white or Cremnitz white) is the fastest-drying of the whites and, in addition, it has the best covering power. A paint with a long history, it was used in China and in the earliest European paintings. According to Mr. Bocour, white lead has a bad reputation that is completely unwarranted. "Sulphur fumes, which have been publicized as being destructive to lead, rarely come in contact with paintings. Further, the toxic effect of lead is dangerous mostly in the handling of dry pigment." When asked to explain the difference between flake-white artists' color and commercial house-paint white lead, for example, Mr. Bocour listed some short-comings of the latter product for artistic use. The excess oil (which can be poured off), plus the use of second-grade dark oil in grinding, rapidly discolors this white. It may be appropriate for grounds but not for actual painting. In contrast to lead, zinc white is slower-drying and has less covering power. "Wide areas covered with zinc tend to become brittle and may crack." The newest white, titanium dioxide, has been improved since its introduction; at the beginning Mr. Bocour felt it was "too chalky." Titanium is the whitest of the three whites.

Next, earth colors were discussed. "Earth colors," Mr. Bocour said, "actually come out of the earth. For some reason people find this hard to believe." But earth colors, as Mr. Bocour rightly insisted, are in fact obtained from the earth. They are formed by iron oxide "staining" the earth. Since this natural process varies a great deal, the umbers, ochers, and siennas tend to vary also. The earth colors are permanent, but they are not as fast-drying as the artificial iron-oxides — the Mars colors. Mars colors are produced in black, brown (a chocolate tone), violet (a dull violet-brown), and yellow (an orange ocher). They grind more easily and mix better than the natural earth colors. (It should be noted that Mr. Bocour was among the first to introduce these useful pigments.) Comparing Mars black to ivory black, Mr. Bocour noted that Mars dries more consistently, with less danger of shiny and dull spots. In addition, ivory black is "cooler" and extremely slow-drying. The ivory black originally used by the old masters was made by burning chips of ivory; now "ivory" black is just a name, for the pigment at the present time is made from charred bones. "If it were still made from ivory," Mr. Bocour commented, "there would not be enough elephants to supply the artists in New York City for one day."

The cadmiums (yellows, reds, and orange) which were next discussed are chemically produced from a durable metal. The cadmium colors, commercially introduced in America in 1917, replace the chrome colors and vermillion, for, although the vermillion used in ancient China has not faded, most grades available today turn black. Mr. Bocour continued with comments on violet pigments: "Cobalt violet is most popular. It was previously composed of cobalt arsenite — a poisonous material. At present we use cobalt phosphate." Manganese violet is duller, denser, and gives off less light than cobalt. It should be noted that the cobalt and manganese colors are among the fastest drying pigments. The cobalt group also includes a pale greenish-blue (cobalt green) and an almost spectrum cobalt blue. Manganese blue, by contrast, is a transparent, brilliant turquoise color. Brilliant blues and greens are also produced by the Monastral colors, (phthalocyanine) blue and green, which are among the newest additions to the permanent palette.

The discussion turned at this point to problems of manufacturing artists' oil colors. "Take yellow ocher." Mr. Bocour began. "There are dozens of different shades available. But each company can produce only one." The tinting power, mass tones, and ability to mix well with other colors are the factors which are taken into consideration in the final selection. The grinding of the selected shade poses another problem. "Each pigment has a different personality and temperament, and must be treated differently in the grinding process." In the grinding stage a binder is added to prevent separation of the oil and pigment. In the Bocour professional line of colors, beeswax is employed, while in *Bellini* the binder is aluminum stearate. When asked if aluminum stearate is also a "filler," Mr. Bocour explained that aluminum stearate costs fifty cents a pound and yellow ochre considerably less. "If I wanted just a filler, I'd use clay." This led to a comparison of so-called student-grade and artist-grade colors. "The difference is best illustrated by cadmium colors. In my student grade, *Bellini*, cadmium-barium is employed; barium being the inert filler. C.P. (chemically pure) cadmium used in *Bocour* has two or three times the tinting power." The difference in the earth colors is a "stronger concentrate."

Last of all, Mr. Bocour talked of the possible development of future media. The synthetic resins, in Mr. Bocour's opinion, seem better than the natural resins. "According to scientific tests, when they age they don't discolor. The house-paint industry must be congratulated for developing these new resins which are gradually being tried by the painter."

From the above, one may see that the problem of the permanent palette is both complex and constantly changing. It behooves the serious painter to be aware of the basic facts of the durability and drying properties of his pigments, as well as to be open to new technological developments in the field.

There follows below a summary of the permanent palette as it stands at the present time.

A Basic Permanent Palette:

WHITE: flake (lead) , zinc, titanium

YELLOW: cadmium, Naples, zinc, Hansa, ocher

BLACK: mars, ivory

RED: cadmium, alizarin, mars, Indian, Venetian red

BROWN: burnt umber, raw umber, burnt sienna, raw sienna, mars

BLUE: ultramarine, cobalt, cerulean, maganese, pthalocyanine (monastral)

GREEN: viridian, chromium oxide, terre verte, phthalocyanine (monstral) , permanent (a mixture) , cobalt

VIOLET: cobalt, manganese, mars (a reddish brown)

17.   Tour of the Grumbacher Factory

Paints and Brushes

Although these days the artist himself seldom prepares his own oil paints, and does not make his own brushes, he may gain insight into what are the desirable properties of these tools by knowing something of their production.

Grumbacher is one of the most noted American producers of artists' supplies. What follows is a report of a tour that the author made of the Grumbacher factory, located on two large floors of a New York loft building. Although Grumbacher produces a great variety of materials, the following is primarily concerned with the production of oil paints and brushes.

The tour started with the production of oil paints. Several large mills are used to grind vast amounts of varying shades of cadmium red. The pigment and the various oils are weighed out and dumped into a large vessel and the vessel placed under a mixer which stirs the ingredients. This "rough mix" is then put into the back of the mill and ground. When the color comes off the mill it is checked for shade, brilliance, and consistency. The pigment is then put back into the mill and ground again. Usually this is sufficient, and the pigment is placed in a smaller container, covered to keep out the air, and stored for aging. This aging process allows the medium to saturate the pigments completely. The amount of oil used in mixing is so carefully controlled that very seldom will any of it "sweat" to the surface.

The three-roller mills employed are water-cooled, for a

High speed three roller mill for grinding the color. Rollers are water cooled to prevent heat. Gauges control pressure to exact amount required for best grinding. Grinding is done on two bottom rollers, top roller picks up the finely ground color where a doctor blade picks it off. The color accumulates on the chute and slides into the pot.

The tails of the red tartar marten — the hair cut from the tail in small clumps — the scissors for cutting hair from the tail — the comb for cleaning out wool and tangled hair from the clumps — the knife used in picking out broken and turned hairs — the hairs assorted in size — bundles of perfect hair ready to be made in brushes — some finished brushes.

machine which is not so cooled is apt to "burn" the pigments. At Grumbacher's the mills have pressure gauges which ensure equal grinding at both ends of the large rollers. Each final run produces up to sixty gallons of pigment which, after aging and testing, is emptied into a group of small containers. These are taken to the tubing department, where they are connected to a feeding device which injects an exact amount of paint into tubes rotating below. The final operation is the testing again of each batch of pigment for tone and consistency.

Every company produces so-called standard colors which differ slightly from products of other companies; there are many sources of supply for natural earth pigments, and the chemically produced colors naturally vary from manufacturer to manfacturer. A company must produce a color with the knowledge that it can repeat the exact color in the future; the control must be constant. Unique colors produced by Grumbacher which the author feels are particularly useful include the following: thio violet, an alizarin-type transparent crimson-violet; golden alizarin, an alizarin processed to produce a warm red-brown; manganese violet, a heavy, opaque, dark, fast-drying violet; and permanent bright green, a cold, intense, opaque green.

The production of brushes, which takes place on a separate floor, is a much more complicated procedure than might be imagined. Upon entering the brush-making department, for example, one is confronted with a complicated Rube Goldberg type of machine, with belts revolving on two levels; this was created by Grumbacher to blend, comb, and clean the various bristles and hairs used in brushes. Skunk, squirrel, and ox hairs in various combinations are thoroughly mixed to produce one uniform color and texture.

Red-sable brushes are hand-produced in a series of delicate operations. Tufts of hair are shaved from the tails of red sables (Tartar martens) and graded according to five or six sizes. The tips of the tails possess the longest hairs, but the best points come from the center. After grading, the hairs are submerged in water, allowed to dry, and then baked in an oven for thirty-six hours at two hundred degrees — a process which stiffens each hair. The last operation in preparing a brush point is called "knifing"; small bundles of hair are tested for resilience with a steel comb, and strands of hair that are too wild or unmanageable are extracted with a knife. More than half of the hairs are discarded in this intricate procedure; only the soft tips remain.

Small metal cups whose inner shapes correspond to the exact negative of the desired brush are employed to form each of the various types. These negative shapes range from long and pointed to flat and stubby — in short, all the possible traditional shapes. The groups of hairs thus moulded are snapped into metal ferrules with what sounds like a sudden clicking of fingers. These brushes, as yet without handles, are transported to another section where resin (nylox) is poured into the top of the ferrules to glue the tops of the hairs together. To ensure adhesion, the glue is "set" by heat, the brushes being baked again, this time for four hours at 375 degrees. The final procedure, "crimping," is the fastening of wooden handles to the ferrules by a machine which firmly stamps the metal ferrule around the wood.

At the end of this brush-making tour, I was asked to compare an imitation sable, made from ox hair and tinted to match red sable, with the genuine product. The sable brush seemed much more obedient to the touch and snapped back to its original shape after each stroke. The imitation, by contrast, seemed to resist; consequently, it would be harder to maneuver on the canvas or paper.

This ended the main part of the tour, but there were interesting sidelights. I observed colored ink in large glass containers being filtered through layers of filter paper and learned that the ink is composed of dyestuff, shellac, and water. And pastel sticks were being produced from gums and pigment: soft sticks were ejected from gunlike machines and set aside to dry. Finally, I discussed the production of dammar varnish with Grumbacher's chemist, Willy Nusinoff. The standard formula — "a five-pound cut" — means five pounds of dammar crystals to each gallon of turpentine. To make a pint: six and a quarter ounces by weight to ten fluid ounces. The crystals, contained in a transparent cloth bag, are suspended in the turpentine. Grumbacher makes dammar in huge containers, which are periodically agitated to stimulate dissolution. Finally, the solution is strained through cheesecloth and bottled.

There is one primary result of a tour of a factory like Grumbacher. The artist gains a heightened respect for those materials he is apt to take for granted.

18.   Grounds and Supports for Painting

In the sixteenth century Vasari transcribed the following recipe for preparing an oil painting for canvas: "In order to be able to convey pictures from one place to another, men have invented the convenient method of painting on canvas, which is of little weight and when rolled up is easy to transport. Unless these canvases intended for oil painting are to remain stationary, they are not covered with gesso, which would interfere with their flexibility, because the gesso would crack if they were rolled up. A paste, however, is made of flour and of walnut oil with two or three measures of white lead put into it, and after the canvas has been covered from one side to the other with three or four coats of smooth size this paste is spread on by means of a knife and all the holes come to be filled up by the hands of the artist. That done, he gives it one or two more coats of soft size, and the composition of priming." *

Obviously, the preparation of an oil ground (here used to include both sizing and oil coating) has not changed radically to this day. Sizing is intended to act as a thin, uniform coating to prevent oil from coming into direct contact with the canvas. But slight mistakes in following established practices can cause disastrous results. For example, glue sizing which is not thinned enough with water causes buckling and cracking. If gelatin is employed for sizing it should be thinned to twelve parts water to one part glue; rabbitskin glue should be thinned at least to a ten-to-one proportion — preferably twelve-to-one.

The oil ground should be spread evenly and should be thin enough to expose the texture of the canvas. The composition of the ground is also important; although most technical experts

---

*Translated by Louisa Maclehose. Quoted by A. P. Laurie, *The Painter's Methods and Materials* (Lippincott, Philadelphia, 1926).

feel that commercially prepared white-lead pastes, such as Dutch Boy are adequate, it must be noted that the oil used in these products is not so refined as the oil used in the manufacture of artists' colors, and that the former will yellow in a relatively short period. However, a mixture of one part Dutch Boy to one part flake white (also lead) or zinc white (artists' color) will not yellow as much. It is a mistake to thin the priming coat with oil; a ground should be lean, that is, relatively oil-free. Turpentine or turpentine with varnish is safer than oil.

Here are some simple rules for stretching, isolating, and priming canvas: Do not stretch the unprimed linen too tightly over the stretcher for the glue may tighten it so much that it twists the stretcher. Apply the glue economically, working out the contents of each brush-full; barely cover the surface — do not let the glue soak through the fabric. Be economical in applying the grounds as well.

A ground prepared by the artist has advantages. It is less absorbent; a thin wash with turpentine stays on the surface, remaining transparent and reflecting the white undercoat. And color generally is more brilliant against this ground, which resists the paint.

Gesso, as noted by Vasari, is too brittle for canvas. A slight jolt will readily cause cracks. But an addition of about 25% boiled linseed oil to the gesso mix, when it is being heated and stirred, produces a half-chalk ground, the oil making the ground flexible enough to apply to the canvas. It should be added, though, that experts are divided as to its permanence. Synthetic resin emulsion gesso, which is also flexible enough to bend with canvas (or paper) without cracking, is now available and seems — according to every test except time — to be satisfactory. Permanent Pigments' Liquitex, Utrecht Linens' New Temp, and Museum Artist Materials' Quick-On are gessoes that may be applied directly to canvas (or panel) without a prior sizing. These products produce on canvas extremely absorbent grounds which transform the normally shiny surface of oil paints into a relatively flat surface. But there is a danger that the oil may pene-

J. M. W. Turner, English, 1775-1851. *The Slave Ship*. Oil. Museum of Fine Arts, Boston. Turner employed a pure white ground. Painters who have been observing Turner's paintings for years insist that his pictures are becoming increasingly brilliant.

trate the ground and stain the canvas. If an absorbent ground is not desired when using these products, one should isolate the surface of the canvas with turpentine and dammar varnish or with another resin.

A ground composed of two layers, plastic gesso and lead-oil paste, is particularly recommended. (To repeat, the plastic gesso does not require sizing.) In this case, the gesso's brilliant white surface demands only a very thin oil covering, which should be applied and scraped carefully with a spatula or a palette knife.

Among painters who employ canvas as a support, a common complaint is the quality of commercial wooden stretchers. Painters must select their stretchers carefully, for warping of the sticks is far too common. Consequently, a great many professional artists construct their own stretchers — painters today, it seems, must also be good carpenters. However, for those who wish to purchase stretchers, the painter, Milton Goldring (172 Bleeker Street, New York City) supplies large-size sturdy strips at a reasonable price.

The alternative to canvas as a support is a panel. Masonite, a type of fiber building-board made from wood chips of yellow pine, is widely employed and recommended. It comes both tempered and untempered, the latter being preferred because it is not coated with oil. In the western hemisphere, wood panels have been employed in painting since early Egyptian history. A partial list of the variety of woods, that has been used since the early Renaissance, would include beech, cedar, fir, chestnut, poplar, mahogany, oak, and olive. The wood must be seasoned and expertly braced. Plywood usually cracks and should be avoided unless it is covered with canvas; the canvas must be soaked in glue size and the panel kept under weights until dry.

Gesso has proved to be the best — and least expensive — ground for panels. Gesso originally referred to plaster of Paris and glue water, but a typical formula today gives equal amounts (by volume) of zinc white (powder), whiting, and glue water.

Paper, too, has been employed for oil painting as well as for water media: there is an oil sketch on paper by Memling in the Louvre. The paper (100% rag) should be coated with a very thin glue solution. Dry pigment may be mixed with the glue to produce an all-over ground color.

Grounds on all supports are usually white, and there seems to be considerable justification for this. In his treatise, written in 1586, Giovanni Battista Armenin stated that paintings with dark grounds ultimately darken. And Max Doerner has warned that the ground has an extraordinary influence on the durability of the picture and the action of colors, as well as on the later preservation and luminosity of the painting. As the oil film is thinned by time, the ground is thereby exposed. Painters who have been observing Turner's paintings for years insist that his pictures are becoming increasingly brilliant. Turner employed a pure white ground — a fact that should be kept in mind.

19.   The Final Varnish

Andrew Petryn

Should all paintings be varnished? Is there one resin best for all paintings? These are the sorts of questions which prompted the author to interview Andrew Petryn, conservator of paintings at the Yale Gallery. At the time, Mr. Petryn was in the process of coating a painting which he later used to demonstrate some of the optical problems involved.

First of all, Mr. Petryn condemned the used of varnish as a panacea: "Never rely on the application of varnish to hold the picture together visually, for its effect may not be lasting. I seriously doubt that all the old masters varnished their paintings to achieve the desired completed effect. For example, Tintoretto or Tiepolo did so many paintings that it is hard to imagine that they would have had time to wait for a final varnish. The painting medium of these masters was probably rich enough (i.e., high percentage of resin oil) to make varnishing unnecessary." The actual binding media used by the old masters are not fully known, Mr. Petryn explained; the proportion of resin to oil or the type of oil used as a medium cannot be determined with certainty. Moreover, it would be a mistake to try to duplicate the present surface of an old painting with the thought that this would offer a key to past techniques; the process of oxidation is constantly going on, and therefore, the appearance of an oil painting is always changing.

But despite these warnings, Mr. Petryn did list three reasons for varnishing paintings: first, a varnish offers a limited protection from moisture and temperature change; second, dirt will remain on the surface of the varnish rather than on the painting; third, the original optical character is, within limits, restored to old surfaces. Ideally, a varnish should be easily removed without damage to the painting. Above all, the rules of good craftsmanship must be followed, for poor application of quality material obviously can do harm to a painted surface. Therefore each resin, natural or synthetic, must be experimented with, for the formulas are endless, and no one varnish or surface coating can be used for every painting.

Before listing the actual resins employed, Mr. Petryn displayed a recently varnished egg-tempera panel. "The key to varnishing is the painter's optical intention. In this painting the quality of the medium, as well as the optical intent, would be violated if a glossy surface were applied — for the medium's inherent beauty would be destroyed. In oil, varnishing is more difficult because a variety of optical effects is possible — ranging from semi-mat to very shiny. The conservator is therefore responsible for making the decision about the optical intention of the painter. Naturally, for the living painter, the problem is different. Instead it is the knowledge of available materials which can create the desired effect."

We returned to the materials, beginning with the natural resins, dammar and mastic. Dr. Robert L. Feller, Fellow of the Mellon Institute of Industrial Research, who has been carrying out exhaustive tests on all types of varnishes, reported in 1951 that "tests under ultraviolet light indicate that the natural resins, yellow to begin with, tend to increase in yellowness with age." Comparing the natural resins, dammar and mastic, to polyvinyl acetate and polybutyl methacrylate, Dr. Feller added that "these particular synthetics are clear and are highly resistant to yellowing." Yet these plastics are not without problems, for Dr. Feller has recently warned of the possibility of certain plastics "losing their solubility under the action of intense heat and

Partially cleaned painting — attributed to Piero di Cosimo: *Portrait of a Lady with a Rabbit*, circa 1506-1509, Tempera on wood, 23″ x 17⅝″ Jarves collection. Yale University Art Gallery.

light." But he added, "This particular problem does not appear to be unsolvable."

Mr. Petryn credited Rutherford J. Gettens and George L. Stout* as being among the first to experiment with plastics for final varnishes. The most widely used plastics, poly normal-butyl methacrylate [Rohm and Haas], poly isobutyl methacrylate [Du Pont], and polyvinyl acetate [Union Carbide, Bake-

---

*Authors of *Painting Materials, A Short Encyclopedia* (D. Van Nostrand Co., New York, 1942) .

lite Division], make many surface effects possible. Various degrees of matness and glossiness can be produced with different solvents. This is where experimentation is necessary, for in Mr. Petryn's words, the conservator or artist must "tailor-make" the optical effect. He was therefore somewhat reluctant to give definite formulas. But he did mention certain solvents for the synthetic resins: xylene, petroleum thinners, and acetone are employed for poly (butylmethacrylate), and ethyl alcohol and toluene for poly (vinylacetate), the solvent usually comprising at least 60 to 70% of the varnish. These synthetics may be employed in combination, that is, one can be sprayed on top of another (after the lower coat is thoroughly dry), and both may be either brushed or sprayed. For spraying it is necessary to use a spray gun which gives a steady, even pressure and has a fine nozzle.

Mr. Petryn severely warned that the solvents may be toxic. "They should be used with a maximum of ventilation. Needless to add, avoid smoking."

Plastic varnishes specially prepared for artists' use include the following: Synvar and Unvar [F. Weber Co.], Rembrandt Picture Varnish [Talens and Sons], and Magna Picture Varnish [Bocour]. Mr. Petryn suggested that the artist using these products write to the manufacturer for complete information and instructions. For more general problems he suggested contacting the conservation department of a museum, for it is his opinion that conservators generally will be happy to try to help painters. Dr. Feller, for example, has written: "I look upon my job, not to recommend any particular varnish or resin, but to describe the various types. The more we seek to measure and describe their properties, the better the artist will be able to make a selection to suit his own needs."

In summary, the painter who employs a varnish should be aware of its particular optical effect. The problems involved are complex, and no one varnish or procedure can meet every need. The new plastics demand individual experimentation, which should be based on consultation with the company that makes the product.

PART TWO: SCULPTURE

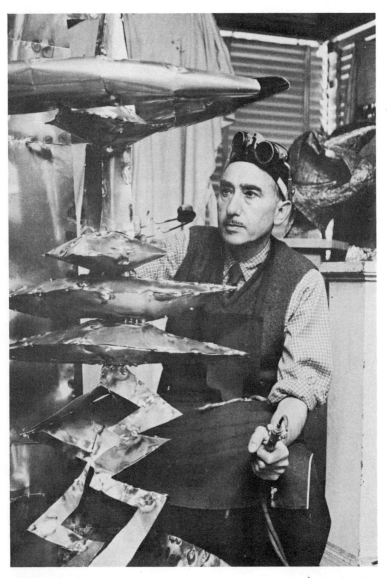

Seymour Lipton at work.

20.　Direct Metal Sculpture

Seymour Lipton

Seymour Lipton, a pioneer in direct metal sculpture, was chosen to have a one-man show at the Venice Biennale in 1958. He was also represented at the Brussels World's Fair. International interest in his sculpture has been paralleled by a growing interest in his personal direct-metal technique. In an interview with the author he discussed his unique working process: "Increasingly during the past four years I have been creating small metal armature models as studies for full-scale sculpture. I found that a drawing did not provide enough of a basis for critical judgment — after all, you can't turn a drawing around." He then displayed some of his schematic working drawings, on which the armature models are based; these drawings are composed of continuous, unmodulated, broad crayon line. Each of the working drawings that is ultimately chosen has been based on a series with a particular theme: "The source material largely involves biology, technology, and art ideas of the past."

With a drawing before him Lipton begins to construct the model by cutting patterns with heavy shears out of a thin-gauge sheet of monel metal, three feet by eight feet. He bends and fashions these shapes with pliers in a manner he feels is analogous to that of a fashion designer who pins together paper patterns for a dress. He spot-brazes the joints at the chosen intersections, as the patterns are placed end to end. This is accomplished with an oxyacetylene torch. During the working process of cutting, bending, and joining, the relationships in the original drawing are changed and transformed — for the process itself produces judgments and decisions. The model, generally about twelve inches long, may at this stage serve as the basis for a larger piece, or in some cases the model itself may be ultimately developed in three additional stages through which his full-scale sculpture is worked and reworked.

When the formal relationships of this small model armature are satisfactory, it serves both as a basis for further study and a guide for the final, larger, complete sculptural resolution. The final work begins, Lipton feels, when he gauges the scale appropriate to the form; it usually ranges between two and eight and one-half feet.

The method for creating an armature for final works repeats the process of the model, that is, cutting, shaping, and brazing. It was at the completion of the large armature that I first saw *Reef Queen* (shown here in its final stage). The single layer of shiny Monel metal, quite thin, was spot brazed at numerous points; the metal was light enough to allow individual sections to be bent at will. The next stage — melting one-eighth inch rods of bronze (nickel-silver is also frequently employed) with an oxyacetylene flame on the monel metal — created a new surface, adding strength and a sensuous textural surface. These rods melt "like sealing wax" and fuse with the metal. However, the hot coating frequently distorts the metal and it must be hammered back into its original shape.

The next stage further aids the structural strength at the same time as it modifies the form. New patterns of monel metal are cut to form what Mr. Lipton calls "the insides of forms." A duplicate for each existing shape is cut, set in place, and spot-brazed along the edges to the outside metal. These "inside" forms, like the outside surfaces, are also covered with bronze and are finally joined completely to the outside structure. Each form, then, is composed of four layers: two parallel monel-metal patterns, and bronze on the inside and outside surfaces. In this last process — that of adding the second layer of monel and of attaching it — modifications of the form take place at the edges as the sculptor creates modulating thicknesses by controlling the brazing and flow of melting bronze. In *Reef Queen* one can see this control in the turning edges of the central forms.

This ended the strictly technical side of our interview, but Lipton strongly emphasized that "style and technique are ulti-

Seymour Lipton: *Reef Queen,* 1957. Nickel-silver on Monel Metal, 42″ long.
Collection Mr. & Mrs. Maremont, Chicago, Ill.

mately inseparable in the general development of creativity." Through trial and error with many materials and techniques, he has arrived at his present technical method which he believes answers his varied needs as an artist: "Continuing development is a process of locating stylistic and formal solutions adequate to one's complex personal views of art and nature. This process of retentions and rejections led me to explore, among other things, planal forms and the insides of forms." Inside and outside form relationships, combined with flat, convoluting, and pointing forms in endless juxtapositions, comprise the basis for Mr. Lipton's present style, which has come to be associated with organic images related to various symbolic levels of meaning and suggestion.

In this search for form-symbols, Lipton is inspired by "nature, machinery, artifacts, and the human figure," and he does not hesitate to use photographs of tropical vegetation and marine life. "Ultimately," the sculptor explained, "I am trying to create *non-obvious* symbols because they stimulate challenging search in both sculptor and viewer."

SEYMOUR LIPTON, *a native New Yorker born in 1903, was educated at Columbia University. Veteran of numerous one-man shows, including exhibits at the A.C.A. Gallery, Gallerie Et. Etienne, Betty Parson Gallery, Watkins Gallery (Washington, D.C.), and New Paaltz College, he has also appeared in the Museum of Modern Art's "12 Americans" and the Venice Biennale, as well as in other group shows in museums all over the world. His works are in collections of the Metropolitan, Whitney, Santa Barbara, and Brooklyn Museums, the Museum of Modern Art, Albright Art Gallery (Buffalo), Wadsworth Atheneum (Hartford), Munson-Williams-Procter Institute, Yale Gallery, and Sao Paulo Museum, among others. Mr. Lipton, who has works commissioned for Inland Steel Building (Chicago), Manufacturers Trust Company (New York), Franklin Institute (Philadelphia), and a number of synagogues, is the recipient of awards from the Chicago Art Institute, Sao Paulo Biennale, and Institute of Arts and Letters. He is represented by the Betty Parsons Gallery.*

21.   Industrial Sand Casting in Bronze

Leonard Baskin

Leonard Baskin's oversized woodcuts have gained him an impressive reputation as a graphic artist since he first began to exhibit in 1949. Throughout this period he has also been active as a sculptor — carving wood and stone, and casting in bronze — but his sculpture has only recently gained the interest of a wide audience. An understanding of his casting technique may not add to appreciation of his work nor explain his choice of form, but it does explain the limitations of form which this technique like every other technique imposes. And these limitations are not immediately discernable when viewing the sculptures.

The horizontal photograph on next page shows a group of bronzes — variations on a theme of "Dead Man." These bronzes vary as to surface texture; some are shiny and smooth, some such as the larger central bronze are pitted and stained. Although Baskin does rework his bronzes with various tools, his whole process will become clarified as we grasp the nature of bronze industrial sand casting. To simplify matters even further, it would be best to study his sculptural style in general, for that style is the basis of the choice of industrial casting as a technique.

The late Francis Henry Taylor, in an introduction to the catalogue of Baskin's first sculpture show at the Worcester Museum (November 1956) wrote: "Having had opportunities to study abroad, particularly in Italy, where he was deeply influenced by the sculpture of the early Middle Ages and the Trecento, he has brought to his work a sense of humanistic understanding and perception of the inherent tragedy in the art of that country." Mr. Taylor's comments give us an image of

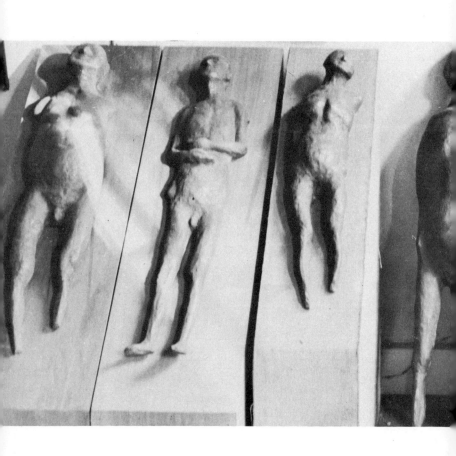

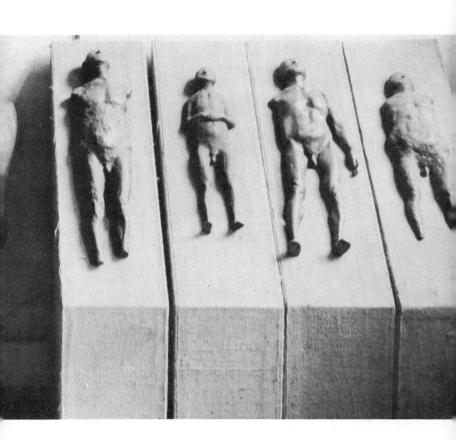

Leonard Baskin: Bronzes. The largest figure is 4' high.

Baskin's visual and philosophical approach. A majority of his sculptures are figures — standing and reclining — and heads. Plastically, each sculpture is composed around a relatively simple core. Sand casting allows no major protruding forms or extensions around this central core. To use the sculptor's vocabulary, there can be no "undercuts." This is the key to the process itself, and Baskin's own sculptural style was one that did not have to be transformed for industrial sand casting in bronze.

In contrast to traditional sculpture casting, in which a plaster mold is made from the original clay or plaster and subsequently recast in sections (separate casts for each extending form), industrial casting demands no preparatory mold or section casts. Instead, the one-step sand-casting method is done directly from the original clay or plaster at a cost which is only a fraction of that involved in traditional methods. For example, Baskin's sculpture is cast by a foundry worker in his off hours. (Industrial sand casting is used commercially to reproduce simple machine parts.)

Let us proceed to a step-by-step description of the process which Mr. Baskin employs. The original clay sculpture, prepared without armatures, is allowed to dry for about a week until it is brittle. Bronze is melted in a crucible in preparation for the simple yet delicate process which produces the sand mold. The sand mold itself is made in two sections. The molding flask, a square structure open at both ends, is composed of two identical empty wooden squares which can be locked together. One of the two sections of the flask is placed on a table, so that if a head, for example, is to be cast, it is placed face down in the center of this half of the flask. Sand, in combination with moist clay to bind it, is shaken in until it completely covers the clay and fills the entire volume of the wooden structure. The sand is carefully compressed until this section of the flask is so tightly and fully packed that one can turn it upside down. This is the next step in the process, at which point the dried clay original is now entirely hidden in the sand. The sand is next delicately cleared away to reveal the sculpture and, of course, it is the face

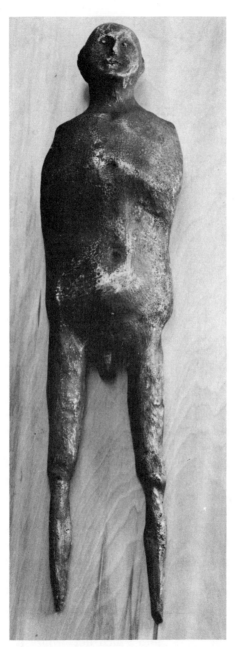

Leonard Baskin: Detail from previous picture

which will be revealed. The clearing away is done with spoon-shaped molder's tools.

Baskin's explanations help one to follow the process. "The crucial theoretical principle is that the clay sculpture must be able to be pulled out of the sand without disturbing the sand mold. A ball is a classic example." The two equal parts of the flask contain equal halves of the ball; the clay head in this case represents the ball. Now let us return to the half-exposed clay head.

Next, the second half of the flask is also packed with sand and placed on top of its counterpart. The sand is gently tapped so that it fills in to touch the exposed clay face below. Now sand from the upper half of the flask tightly surrounds this face in the lower flask. The two halves of the flask are locked together and again flipped over. The head is now face down. The upper section of the flask is unlocked and removed, revealing the back of the head (half the imaginary ball). The flask removed contains the sand negative of this part of the form.

We see now that the face is hidden in the sand, that is, half the sculpture is hidden in the lower flask (again, half the classic ball). The difficult task, already alluded to, is to remove the head without disturbing the sand. When it is accomplished, the second half of the mold is revealed. A complete negative of the clay has been made in two equal sections. And so begins the final stage in casting — the pouring of the bronze.

Before the two sections of the flask containing these molds are locked together, a "core" is suspended in the negative areas of the sand to prevent the bronze from becoming a solid piece. Made of linseed oil and sand, this pre-baked core is propped on light brass pins. Now the sculpture will be hollow. Baskin explains: "In sand casting it cannot be a fine or exact core but merely a simple shape which displaces bronze. The core holds long enough to allow the bronze to set, and then, it disintegrates."

To return to the locked flask with its now suspended core: a hole is tunneled into the flask until it touches the impression. The hole is the "gate" into which hot bronze is poured. In a

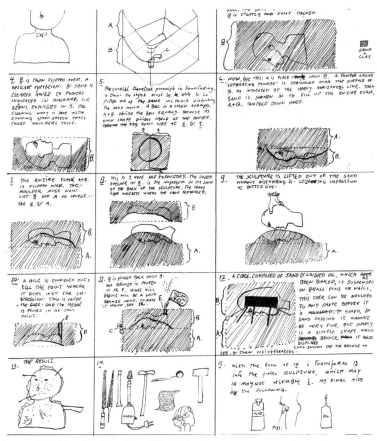

Leonard Baskin: Explanation of Sand Casting process sent to the author.

half-hour the bronze cools and may be removed. Although the casting process is complete, the sculpture itself is not, for the seam in the flask shows on the newly cast bronze. There may be other rough spots as well. The entire bronze may be partly or wholly remodeled — depending on the sculptor's evaluation.

In this final stage Baskin may employ any of the following tools: hack saw, cold chisel, files, an electric grinding machine with abrasives, or a planishing hammer which can beat out ridges as it creates texture. Various açids and oils may be employed at the very end. This last refinishing stage may be the point where a number of sculptors will lose interest in this process; many sculptors do not like to rework bronze. When asked about the difficulty of refinishing bronze, Baskin informed us that bronze is a relatively sóft metal. In fact, he told us, "Zadkine completely carved a bronze block."

The reworking of the bronze in this final phase brings the surface of the sculpture to life through this direct recarving of details. For Leonard Baskin it has become a process in which the original idea can be reinforced — or even transformed. His style, as we have seen, permits the use of the industrial sandcasting process; and his willingness to accept a yet unfinished product permits him to employ his favorite technique. Perfection is achieved by carving, for the artist stays with his creation to the very last instant of the process.

LEONARD BASKIN *was born in New Brunswick, N.J. in 1922 and studied at New York School of Architecture and Allied Arts, Yale University School of Art and Architecture, New School Academie de la Grande Chaumiere (Paris), and Academy of Fine Arts (Florence). At present on the staff of Smith College, he has also taught at Worcester Museum School. Mr. Baskin's works have been exhibited in one-man shows in Florence (Italy), the Little Gallery (Princeton, N.J.), Mt. Holyoke College, Fitchburg Art Museum, Worcester Art Museum, Boris Mirski Gallery, and Grace Borgenicht Gallery, and in group showings throughout the United States and Europe. Winner of numerous awards, from the Brooklyn Museum, Library of Congress, International Society of Wood Engravers, Zurich, Switzerland, among others, Mr. Baskin is represented in over 30 collections, including the Boston Museum of Fine Arts, Brooklyn Museum, Seattle Museum, Worcester Art Museum, Smith College Museum, New York Public Library, Fogg Museum, and Princeton University Library. His agents are the Grace Borgenicht Gallery in New York and the Boris Mirski Gallery in Boston.*

22. Structural Sculpture

Robert Engman

Robert Engman, whose sculpture is related to Constructivism in its economical presentation of form, began his interview with the author by discussing Constructivism: "Traditional Constructivists have merely utilized the principle of Constructivism to arrange predetermined parts into some sort of an esthetic whole." Engman, who prefers to call his own work "structural," differs from the Constructvists in two respects. First, the forms he creates are dependent on the material employed. Second, he produces what he considers organic sculpture — as opposed to machinelike. To clarify his definition of organic he offered an analogy: "Pondering the shape of an oak leaf, one may wonder why it has that particular shape. But if one studies its vascular and cellular structure, one discovers that the peripheral description of this leaf is a consequence of that particular cellular and vascular structure, which in turn relates to the total structure of the tree. I therefore interpret *organic* to mean that all parts are dependent and consequential upon the total form."

Engman extended his definition further: "Particular forms relate to particular materials." The material employed is essential to his concept of form-making. Working with the "nature

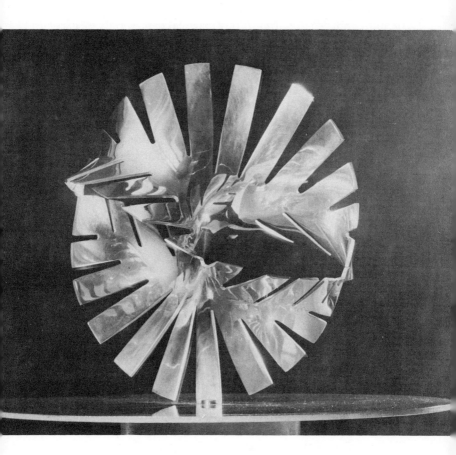

Robert Engman: *The Sun.* Muntz Metal. Collection Mrs. Ira Wallach.

of the material" produces, he feels, an attitude toward form. And to be consistent with his definition of organic, Engman believes he must show the relationship of particular materials to particular forms. He is therefore concerned with the fact that sheet materials have different property from bulk materials, such as stone or wood. Sheet materials have a variety of innate structures; steel, for example, is conducive to different three-dimensional structures than those of paper. This attempt to relate the inherent properties of materials to specific forms brings out as well the relationship of concept to material and form: "Sculpture for me is a result of this action." This interrelation of form with material produces sculpture wherein no specific technique is developed. "Too frequently," he emphasized, "technique exists at the expense of form."

Engman separates craft from technique. Craft, he believes, is absolutely essential to the production of sculpture: "A thorough knowledge of craft frees the artist to concentrate on form. The higher the development of craft, the clearer the content of the form becomes. Naturally, an overemphasis on craft at the expense of formal inventiveness, as well as the ineptness of craft to relate formal invention, is in part the destruction of sculpture." As a result of these beliefs he uses a great many different materials: brass, stainless steel, copper, aluminum, nickel-silver, bronze, Monel, and various types of brazing and welding rods.

Tools, for Engman, are an extension of the hand, which is in turn an extension of the mind. He employs hammers, power equipment, and welding apparatus. Tools, he feels, are servants and should not interfere with form-reading. He implied that he avoids texture which divorces itself from form.

The Sun, a recent sculpture of his, was produced from a twenty-inch square sheet of Muntz metal. In this work, the sculptor expanded a square sheet to a maximum dimension with what he considers a minimum effort. He selected Muntz metal because it has a good relationship of copper and zinc which makes it possible for it to be formed cold as well as with heat. The concept was simply to direct the opposing corners toward each other.

In stretching these corners, certain actions occurred which allowed the edges of the square to increase one-third over the original dimension. In order to allow for this expansion, the metal was cut in one-inch separations toward diagonal lines which had been drawn from corner to corner. When the four corners were related — each to its opposite — the logical action was the spreading of these fingerlike strips to accommodate the increase in the outside dimension. The final configuration resulted in the periphery forming two large circles ninety degrees to each other and two circles tangent — also ninety degrees to each other — and forty-five degrees to the main axis of the two peripheral circles.

The cuts were made with a hand saw; the sheet was then formed (hammered) cold over various forming tools made of Babbitt, a combination of zinc and tin. The surface was gradually filed down to a continuous smooth surface, starting with No. 80 grit abrasive cloth and progressing through ten finer cloths.

When questioned about the relationship of his work to mathematics, Engman replied that a mathematician is such only because he affiliates himself with a system of mathematics to define relationships. Engman considers mathematics artistic in thought: "I use a system of three-dimensional organization to define relationships in terms of 'meaningful form.' " Engman prefers to work in a series. He feels this method is consistent with an organic approach wherein one concept leads to another; for this reason he has been reluctant to exhibit individual pieces of sculpture. And although his sculpture does not relate to specific natural images, he prefers to feel they do relate to nature's process.

Born in Belmont, Mass. in 1927, ROBERT ENGMAN *studied at the Rhode Island School of Design and at Yale University School of Art and Architecture, where he now teaches. He has had one-man shows at the Hewlett Gallery of the Carnegie Institute of Technology, and the Stable Gallery (New York). His sculptures are included in the collections of the Container Corporation, Museum of Modern Art, and the Yale Art Gallery. Mr. Engman is represented by the Stable Gallery.*

23.

Direct Wax

Elbert Weinberg

The "lost" in the lost-wax process, as the sculptor Elbert Weinberg explained in an interview with the author, does not refer to a revived secret method. It merely describes the process in which the wax model is melted — and therefore lost — during the casting process. Weinberg is perhaps best known for his wood carvings. But he prefers to make sketches for these carvings in wax — or, as it is called by sculptors, "direct wax." The fact that he makes preparatory sketches in wax — which in themselves are most often finished sculptures — does not imply that he forces wood to resemble wax (which he employs in sheet form). But it does mean that these sheets, the preparation of which we will here describe, have suggested possibilities of flowing forms and attenuated strippings which Weinberg feels are part of the inherent structure of wood. In short, he feels that his wax studies have helped him discover form possibilities in the handling of wood which he otherwise might have neglected. Needless to add, the initial concept produced in wax is transformed during the carving process.

←— Elbert Weinberg: *Angel of Death*, 1958. Wax model, 18″ high. (Bronze in collection of the Whitney Museum of American Art.)

Weinberg is reluctant to begin a wood sculpture which may involve up to six months of work without the specific core of an idea. Yet the waxes are not the initial concept, for Weinberg, who humorously alludes to himself as "over-cautious," produces countless pen-and-ink drawings as a prelude to these small wax studies.

Thus far we have discussed direct wax in connection with Weinberg's preparations for wood carving, but he also considers direct wax a final medium. This phase of his work usually involves working the wax in a slightly larger scale. Weinberg, like many other sculptors who employ wax, enjoys the special qualities of this medium, which aids a direct and fresh handling of texture and detail. As Weinberg detailed for us the preparation of the wax, its advantages and problems, his enthusiasm for this medium, which permits great flexibility and speedy execution and alteration, was evident.

Weinberg began the technical discussion with a description of the material employed — Petrowax, a Gulf product which is a by-product of the manufacture of gasoline. Weinberg buys this material in fifty-pound tins; he finds it a useful and economical substitute (at twenty-five cents a pound) for the refined mixture of beeswax and carnauba waxes which is sold at foundries for two dollars and fifty cents per pound. Petrowax usually comes in transparent form; the sculptor adds the coloring matter. Dry pigment as coloring matter was found by Weinberg to produce an undesirable grainy surface. He now employs a black or brown aniline dye which is added to the wax when it is being heated in a large container prior to being cast into sheets. The casting into long, thin (three-sixteenths of an inch) sheets is accomplished on an oil-slicked marble top (enamel top will do) which is framed in wood. The wax, poured from the pot where it has been warming, must be poured at exactly the correct temperature. If it is too hot it will crack on cooling; if it is too cold it will not pour freely. The sculptor assured us that it takes only

Elbert Weinberg: *Annunciation*, 1953. Bronze. 12″ high.

a little practice to judge the correct temperature. Many sheets are poured in one day. "At times," Weinberg continued, "I add a little motor oil to the wax to give it more plasticity."

These sheets, which are slightly reheated to make them pliable, may be worked with a variety of metal tools which hold heat: screw drivers, dental tools, and a soldering iron to which Weinberg has refitted a copper blade tip. The marks of these tools are revealed in *Angel of Death,* reproduced in the original wax. Also visible in this photograph are small pellets which are rolled from the wax sheets. In *Annunciation,* also reproduced, the figure on the right demonstrates Weinberg's use of the thin wax sheets; the simple yet elegant wrapping of the sheet becomes the figure. And on the angel figure at the left, the upper left tip of the wing is but an eighth of an inch thick. "The preoccupation with thinness," he continued, "is necessary. An old rule in bronze-casting is that thin walls produce the best bronzes. A foundry does not like to cast a thick wall — it is liable to fracture on cooling. Only a very small wax can be solid." (For casting of solid sculpture in sand, see page 111.)

The wax model is presented to the foundry in the exact thickness of the final bronze. If the model is presented in clay or plaster, the foundry must make a gelatin or plaster mold in order to produce a wax for the final casting. Working in wax cuts the considerable expense of this particular process. (In Europe, where casting is less expensive, this would not be a problem.) Yet it is the special handling quality of wax, rather than economy, which is the primary reason Weinberg prefers it. "Some sculptors," Weinberg added, "work in solid wax (which demands a mold) just because they enjoy the plasticity of wax."

"There are hazards in working in direct wax," Weinberg continued. "Should the original wax be destroyed during casting (the bronze could be poured too hot or too cold), and if there is no mold, the work is lost. I can't say I enjoy this gamble. But to repeat, the special effects possible only in wax, the effects, which I detect in Greek, Indian, and African bronzes, prompt me to take the chance."

Finally, Weinberg discussed the problem of working with wax on a large scale. Because an armature is not employed it presents some difficulties. Some sculptors build a wooden buttress to support the wax; others suspend the wax on fine copper wire. The whole structure, including the wire and wood, however, must be transported to the foundry. Toothpicks, matchsticks, and wooden dowels up to a quarter of an inch in diameter may also be employed; they will "burn out" when the wax is cast. The main problem, however, in working wax on a large scale, is to keep the wax walls at a fairly uniform thickness.

To sum up: Weinberg, who employs wax to make preparatory studies for his large wood carvings, also employs wax as a final medium. The thin wax sheets he casts from Petrowax are, in his words, "a basis for my approach to form."

A native of Connecticut where he was born in 1928, in Hartford, ELBERT WEINBERG *attended the Hartford Art School, Rhode Island School of Design, and Yale University School of Art and Architecture. He teaches at Cooper Union. Mr. Weinberg has exhibited in group showings throughout the United States and has also had a one-man show at the Grace Borgenicht Gallery, which is his agent. Winner of the Prix de Rome and a Guggenheim Fellowship, he is represented in collections of the Museum of Modern Art, Whitney Museum, Yale University Art Gallery, and the Addison Gallery.*

PART THREE: GRAPHICS

24.

Etching Techniques

Rudy Pozzati

Rudy Pozzatti: *Bull*, 1957. Etching on zinc, 14½ x 17½".

Today, American printmaking is enjoying a renaissance. Some art critics have complained of overemphasis on technique or surface treatment in the new work; yet this preoccupation with method has produced a new interest in graphic art among scores of young artists. Perhaps these new methods have expanded the range of visual possibilities, thereby attracting new interest. Or, perhaps printmaking reflects a period of experimentation in the visual arts. These aspects were discussed with Rudy Pozzatti, whose etching techniques will be our concern here. According to Mr. Pozzatti, "Prints displaying technique alone are becoming rare. Printmakers are aware that imagery is more important than surface." But he also emphasized that "a technical vocabulary is the background which makes a personal concept possible." And Mr. Pozzatti called on his vast technical knowledge to fulfill his concept for the etching, *Bull*.

The desired image for *Bull* naturally involved certain formal problems which in turn prompted visual and technical decisions. Mr. Pozzatti's usual manner of form-making — rigid shapes and free-flowing lines to present solids, contours, and interspaces — was discarded because it did not fit the needs of content. Instead, a gradual softening of edges of shapes with modulation within these shapes to produce a general fusion of the whole surface was desired. These conceptual demands inspired the following series of operations.

First, the 14½″ by 17½″ zinc plate had its edges filed and its surface cleaned with a mixture of ammonia and whiting (a routine procedure). Next, an irregular aquatint was placed over the entire surface: an aquatint is composed of powdered rosin which is dusted on the heated plate; heat changes the rosin from powder into crystal. In Mr. Pozzatti's words, "The acid, biting around each crystal, produces a characteristic texture." After the aquatint was applied, and before the first acid bath, the shapes and lines which were to appear as light areas were brushed on with stop-out varnish. (Stop-out varnish prevents acid-biting). This first stage, worked from dark to light, involved outlining and slightly dissolving the main black shape. These freely brushed strokes, which printed as white, also established a tilting ground plane. The first aquatint etch was used as a means to set the first tonal values for the main black shape as well as for the bottom frontal plane.

The first test print, then, showed a grayish-black textured shape defined by white brush marks. The problems now were to increase the darks gradually within the frontal shape, to soften its edges, and to strengthen the bottom plane. To accomplish these aims, Mr. Pozzatti brushed on a layer of hard ground which covered the entire plate. Hard ground consists of a half-part powdered rosin, two parts Egyptian asphaltum powder, two parts beeswax, and just enough benzine to dissolve the rosin and wax. This mixture is heated — but not to the boiling point — and strained through cheesecloth. Instead of scratching lines through the hard ground to expose the zinc plate to the acid, he dissolved the ground with benzine, the preferred solvent for hard ground. In this "wash-out" process, as Mr. Pozzatti described it, he applied the benzine with a brush and blotted it gently with cloth. "There is control in this process, rather than accident, for it is possible to control the brush strokes and the blottings." And Mr. Pozzatti found this process to be an economical method to produce darks. But economy was secondary, for the darks in the "wash-out" process produced a blending effect which was of primary concern. The plate was reworked in this manner between three separate acid bitings; the darks were blended and strengthened gradually.

The next stage further increased the weight of the darks as it enriched the texture, but it was mainly concerned with softening the edges. This objective was accomplished in the aquatint manner with large particles of rosin, as well as regular aquatint, to prevent flat biting of the plate and to achieve the pitted quality of an aquatint, making it possible to receive more ink for blacker, richer printing. But even after this second aquatint the range of darks still did not satisfy the artist. Therefore, to intensify the dark areas even more he rolled a thin layer of soft ground on the plane. (Soft ground consists of hard ground and axle grease.) Through this ground lines were then scratched. Mr. Pozzatti explained that a soft ground line is less brittle and spreads more than hard ground. The lines merged into the darks in the final print. These lines were patiently added to create clots of black which read darkest on the left and gradually lighten as one reads from left to right. (The photograph does not show this to advantage.) These final darks made the edges appear softer and brought out the tracery of white lines applied at the beginning. These light lines which seem to come at random support the main form by repeating its boundaries. Further, they attract highlights within the main form, and what is most important their placement prevents the dark shapes from becoming a silhouette.

The soft-ground stage, which was also repeated, brought the print to a conclusion. It must be emphasized again that this print was not intended as a display of virtuoso texture. The complicated methods described were already part of Mr. Pozzatti's vocabulary. And these methods were employed only to fulfill his concept.

_____

RUDY POZZATTI *was born in Colorado in 1925 and studied at the University of Colorado. He has exhibited in group shows throughout the United States and has also had one-man showings at the Martha Jackson Gallery (New York), Art Institute of Chicago, Kansas City Art Institute, Weyhe Gallery, Cleveland Museum of Art, and 18 other museums, colleges, and galleries. He formerly taught at the University of Nebraska and now is on the faculty of Indiana University. Mr. Pozzatti has won awards from the University of Illinois, City Art Museum (St. Louis), Print Club (Philadelphia), and Butler Art Institute (Youngstown, Ohio), in addition to being the recipient of 35 other citations, including a Fulbright Scholarship. He is represented in well over 50 collections, including the Boston Museum of Fine Arts, Brooklyn Museum, City Art Museum, Fogg Museum, Museum of Modern Art, and the Metropolitan. Agents for Mr. Pozzatti's works are the following: Weyhe Gallery (New York) — prints and drawings; Jacques Seligman (New York) — paintings; Forsythe Gallery (Ann Arbor, Mich.), Schermerhorn Gallery (Beloit, Wis.); Gumps (San Francisco); IFA Gallery (Washington, D.C.).*

25.   Color Printing: Paper Relief Cuts

Edmond Casarella

In the past decade American printmaking has been noted for its technical virtuosity. This interest in process directs an artist to compose in terms of the process and its limitations. As innovations have expanded graphic processes, many artists have increasingly devoted their energies exclusively to printmaking. Never before, perhaps, have so many artists been working in this area. Printmaking, it seems, is no longer considered a minor art to be practiced as time-out relief from so-called "major" media.

The interest in color is a major reason for this renaissance. Prints employing an unlimited color range have narrowed the gap between graphics and painting. A criticism, often heard, that prints have become printed paintings may be true in isolated cases, but, for the most part, the prints in color one is apt to see in major exhibitions faithfully reflect graphic processes. This interest in color, however, has produced techniques differing from the traditional color print which employs a key block in black with overprintings in color.

For nine years Edmond Casarella has been working with a method which he calls cardboard or paper relief cuts; his method permits extensive color printing. The technique, primarily based on the woodcut relief process, permits a color conception without distorting graphic ideas. Let us relate the method step by step as Mr. Casarella described and demonstrated it in an interview.

Casarella prepares for a print by producing a "rough" gouache sketch which is translated and in turn transformed in the various stages of producing the blocks or plates. "The construction of the blocks is part of the creative process," Mr. Casarella emphasized. The blueprints for the blocks are the color separations made from the original gouache. These separations are not merely mechanical tracings of the original. Decisions concerning the number of colors on any one block and the juxtaposition of opaque and transparent overlays prompt changes from the original concept; unessential shapes and colors are gradually eliminated. "The separations represent a refining process," Casarella explained. A sheet of tracing paper indicating plans for one block may reveal shapes to be printed in only one color, or it may call for up to six different colors. *Tree Burst* was created with six blocks containing twenty colors. A cardboard plate for *Tree Burst,* reproduced herewith, shows a block that produced three greens and three browns. "Generally," Casarella noted, "in the production of blocks, the largest shapes are considered first."

When the color separations on tracing paper are completed, they indicate the number of blocks to be employed. (Casarella has employed as many as eight blocks holding sixty colors.) Each block is cut from heavyweight chip board to the exact size of the gouache sketch. Next, shapes slightly larger than those traced are drawn and cut from double-weight illustration board and are glued (with rubber cement) into exact position. On these larger shapes, the exact shapes are accurately traced. In short, each exact shape is marked on a slightly larger shape which is pre-cut and glued into position. When each block has been prepared in this manner, the cutting begins. It should be noted here that the tracing paper is reversed so that the print produced is not a mirror image.

Now let us return to the illustration-board shapes glued on to the chipboard base. Casarella scores the exact shape with an industrial single-edge razor blade or a mat knife. He cuts at a

Edmond Casarella: *Tree Burst*. **Paper Relief Cut.**

Edmond Casarella: one plate for *Tree Burst*.

slight angle away from the shape and begins to peel off the excess illustration board. Illustration board, constructed in layers, is easy to peel away; again, this peeling away is not a mechanical procedure, for the artist decides how much to remove, thereby affecting the print. Casarella explained: "I can decide whether to incorporate the second level of the shape by the depth of the cut. If I decide to print the edge of the oversized shape as a secondary shape or ghost, I cut only halfway through the cardboard. If, however, the outer edge is to be discarded, I merely cut down to the chip-board." (The block reproduced here shows the outer edges of the primary shapes cut to different levels.) "Texture," Casarella added, "can be produced by breaking the surface with an ice pick or a nail. But these areas must be reinforced with a surface coating of Elmer's Glue or shellac."

The order of printing the blocks is determined by the color separations. The blocks with the largest shapes, usually in opaque colors, are printed first. "The registering of the paper so that each block appears in the exact position indicated is fairly easy. There are many systems of registry — each artist must find the one most compatible to his working method." Printing inks employed are International Printing Inks and offset industrial ink. Especially useful is I.P.I.'s "transparent white," which is not actually white, but a transparent, jelly-like liquid which can reduce any color to a glaze. When oil inks are employed the blocks do not require a prior coating with glue or shellac. Casarella found that blocks coated with oil inks and cleaned with turpentine were not affected. But water and waterbase ink must be avoided, for water destroys the illustration board. Except for this one precaution, Casarella assured us that cardboard is strong enough to withstand a sizable edition.

Gelatin rollers in different widths are employed for inking the blocks. Casarella has constructed some very small holders for these rollers. He found that any manufacturer of gelatine rollers could easily produce rollers to fit his holders. (They were needed to ink very small areas.) Wooden spoons are employed to hand-rub the ink on the paper. Casarella mixes his color in quantity and prints one block at a time in order of their prominence and in relation to the desired play between opaque and transparent color areas. He allows at least twenty-four hours for each printed block to dry before printing an overlay or an adjacent shape. Paper employed is Mulberry or Troya purchased from Nelson-Whitehead Paper Co. For large prints, he employs a paper which is produced in rolls by the Technical Paper Co. (25 Huntington Ave., Boston, Mass.)

In short, this involved process, which begins with an original gouache and proceeds to color separations, cutting, and peeling, — aside from printing — is not merely a reproductive process. Each stage is part of the creative act. Each stage ultimately affects the final image.

Born in Newark, New Jersey, in 1920, EDMOND CASARELLA *studied at Cooper Union and the Brooklyn Museum School, where he is now a member of the faculty. He is also Art Director of the Sales Presentations Department of American Broadcasting Company. Mr. Casarella has had one-man shows at Zabriskie Gallery (New York), Obelisk Gallery (Washington, D.C.), University of Louisiana, and University of Mississippi. In addition, his works have appeared in group showings throughout the United States and Europe, as well as in a two-man show at the Brooklyn Museum. Winner of several awards — Brooklyn Museum Print Annual (three times), Library of Congress, Philadelphia Print Club, University of Illinois Print Show (twice), Northwest Print Makers, International Water Color Exhibition, Print Council of America, among others. Mr. Casarella is represented in collections of the City Art Museum (St. Louis), Brooklyn Museum, Cincinnati Art Museum, and the De Cordova Museum (Lincoln, Mass.)*

PART FOUR: DRAWING

26.   Drawing Techniques and Formulas

During the Renaissance, drawing was considered analytical investigation and practice for the finished work of art, which was to be executed in another medium. The working drawings of this period, more than the final works, give us an intimate glimpse of the artist's search, for they reveal the initial impulse which gave birth to the concept. To be sure, drawing still serves as a rehearsal for some artists, but since the Renaissance a drawing has come to be considered a work of art in its own right. We have come to admire the individual handwriting that is revealed in drawing, but often hidden in other media. Old-master drawings much admired today, by Rembrandt and Tiepolo for example, reveal a masterly shorthand expression; we witness a personal calligraphy in the service of economical form in space presentation.

A new interest in drawing is evident today — if we may judge from the increase in major exhibitions. "Recent Drawings — U.S.A.," presented at the Museum of Modern Art, 1956, and "Golden Years of American Drawings, 1950-1956," at the Brooklyn Museum, revealed changes in drawing methods and techniques which will be our concern here. For example, mixed-media drawings seem to be rarer than fifty or twenty-five years ago. There is a directness of expression evident — by this I do not mean that much-abused word "spontaneity," but rather a simplification of means. There seems to be less self-conscious mechanical modeling, less smudging. In short, graphic directness, even in very involved drawings, seems to be the major mode. And yet there is a great diversity of instrumentation, content, and compositional means. The directness affects tool marks, which are now more revealed than hidden — even in wash drawings brush strokes seem carefully preserved. There also appears to be a change in drawing tools. Although the various steel pens remain popular, a great variety of other pens is now seen: reed, bamboo, quill, even wooden sticks. Brush is also extremely popular — broad and sweeping, or thin and undulating. This graphic directness can perhaps be traced to contemporary painting. Influential painters such as Pollock, De Kooning, and Kline have employed graphic ideas formerly considered the exclusive province of drawing. On the other hand, the so-called "broad media," chalk and charcoal, seem to be a little less in evidence.

Tools, media, and formulas are the subject of a technically focused book, *The Craft of Old-Master Drawings,* by James Watrous (University of Wisconsin Press, Madison), which bears discussion here. Mr. Watrous includes many practical workshop procedures. Diagrams for cutting reed and quill pens are supplied. A traditional shape — almost that of a steel pen — is recommended for the quill. A quill so cut produces a free-flowing flexible line. If a line varying from very thick to thin is desired, a blunt point which is cut convex on one side and concave on the other is recommended. A very fluid ink is further advised. I would add that Higgins Eternal Black carbon ink works well with this tool. Reeds are generally available, but, if they cannot be obtained, Grumbacher bamboo pens make an excellent substitute.

For those who would like to experiment with ink-making to meet individual tastes and needs, the book gives recipes for blister, iron-gall, and black carbon — the last of which we reproduce:

1. Take eight ounces of water and heat it almost to the boiling point.
2. Remove it from hot plate and add one ounce of rabbitskin glue, stirring until the glue is completely dissolved.
3. Into a mortar place one level tablespoon of lampblack dry color of good quality, such as one may purchase from suppliers of artist's pigments.
4. Add two teaspoons of the hot glue size and work the lampblack into the glue with a pestle. Although the two ingredients do not seem miscible at first, vigorous circular grinding will produce a smooth paste within one or two minutes.
5. Continue the grinding until the mixture is well worked, then add one teaspoon of the hot glue size and work it into the paste.
6. One may then follow one of two procedures in forming the stick or cake of ink:
   a. Pour the mixture into a shallow porcelain or glass receptacle to dry. Although it will not affect the quality of the ink, the stick or cake will crack or warp during the drying process.
   b. Instead, one may pour the cream-thick ink into a receptacle, stirring and working it as the moisture evaporates until it may be pressed into a semisolid stick form. It is then covered, or wrapped in wax paper, and slowly dried throughout.
7. As in the case of Chinese ink sticks, the liquid may be easily prepared to the proper consistency and intensity by rubbing the sticks with a proper amount of water, in a porcelain dish or a slate ink-saucer.

Other highlights in the book are formulas for making crayons, chalks, and toned grounds. Mr. Watrous has also attempted to analyze the tools used in many old-master drawings in American collections. These drawings are well reproduced and the microphotographic enlargements involve the reader in the research. This well-timed book, it is hoped, will add to the public's enjoyment of drawing as a separate art form.

One postscript: despite the new interest in drawing, draftsmen are apt to compain about the collectors' and galleries' primary concern with the so-called major media (some dealers do not handle drawings for lack of storage space). But on the bright side, there appears to be a wholesale exchange of drawings between artists. Perhaps in this way drawing will be preserved even if the recent interest dwindles.

27. Individual Drawing Techniques

Hyman Bloom

At an early age Hyman Bloom produced masterful drawings. In his "teens" he studied the form-building methods of his favorite old masters. These early drawings range from Rubens-like chalk studies of wrestlers to more delicate, precise figure studies in lead pencil. Today, in his forties, he still practices drawing as a separate discipline. But his drawings now reveal a wider scope of technique and an even greater variety of media and drawing tools; he employs gouache, chalk, and charcoal, white ink on toned paper, and dark ink on light paper. Further, he employs what seems to be a combination of these media in one drawing.

Fish, a recent red ("Watteau") Conté-crayon drawing, reveals a seemingly mixed-media work. It is perhaps better described as a mixed-instrument drawing (if there is such a category). Let us explain. The darkest tones at the top have been rubbed with a dry brush to insure a rich, smooth dark. The watery effect at the lower right is created by wetting the already applied Conté surface. The darker brush strokes at the lower left are produced the same way, but with less water. And still other light tones are produced by working into the drawing with kneaded gum eraser. Thus far the technique is not too unusual. But the pen strokes are produced with an "ink" composed of fine Conté-crayon particles and water. These pen strokes can be seen in the upper left; here they gradually blend the darks around the form. Pen marks are also employed to detail the structures within the main forms.

If a foreign color or surface texture produced by a glossy ink were employed, these areas might jump from their spatial position: this unusual "ink" keeps the surface of the drawing consistent. But, according to Bloom in his interview, the prime reason for using this Conté ink is that it permits erasure, thereby insuring a fluid technique.

Of course, gouache, chalk, and charcoal are media which naturally permit desired changes. Yet in another type of Bloom's ink drawings, the white ink on tinted paper mode, he can also "make changes with absolute precision." This is achieved by using a water-soluble white ink which can be "picked up" with a wet cloth or sponge. The tinted ground must of necessity be waterproof. (The inks preferred for this technique are Grumbacher's "Write-White" and an ink made from a poster white, "Dwight White," and water.) Bloom demonstrated this process, first wetting and then blotting the diluted area. Only a faint "ghost" remained. *Beggars* reveals this style with its revisions; the right side of the top of the head, which seems blended, is in reality a "ghost" of one of Bloom's fluid yet surgeon-like operations. One can also detect changes around the hand in the center and in the drapery which surrounds it.

Toned or tinted paper is generally employed with light and dark accents, the background tone assuming the role of the middle value. But Bloom prefers to use white ink alone "and work from the tone of the paper up." Optical grays, however, are produced by the grouping or clotting of the white strokes. And darks surrounded by white ink strokes appear darker than the toned background.

Other drawing styles in which Hyman Bloom works include large, pure Conté drawings and small, rapid pen-and-ink "sketches." The oversize Conté drawings exhibited a few seasons back in his retrospective at the Whitney Museum were intended, we learned, as actual "cartoons" for paintings. He found that transferring these "cartoons" to canvas was a very difficult job at best. And when it was possible to transfer them properly, he found it uninspiring to paint on an already completed vision; there was little margin for development. He jokingly remarked

Hyman Bloom: *Fish*, Red conte crayon.

Hyman Bloom: *Beggars*. White ink on colored ground.

that "cartoons would be practical if an apprentice would do the transferring and the painting."

Bloom's small ink drawings (dark ink on light paper) are composed of long and short darting lines which repeat and change the contours of the form. Here one can witness the changes in structure, posture, and position of the form which would normally be hidden in his white-ink style. These drawings are considered "sketches" as opposed to his other drawings, in which the forms are more clearly defined and the forms are interrelated in an over-all spatial environment.

For one who pursues so many different drawing methods, theories which separate drawing and painting into various categories are of little concern. When pressed for definitions he simply described drawing as "forms without color."

Drawing, then, as practiced by Hyman Bloom, is a separate discipline. He has developed personal techniques which have expanded his visual vocabulary. He works both in a graphic manner — showing each tool mark constructing the form — and in a tonal manner wherein the blending resembles painting. And although he works with many different techniques, his drawings contain the same symbols which have long been identified with his paintings.

HYMAN BLOOM *came to the United States at the age of seven from Lithuania, where he was born in 1913. He studied with Harold Zimmerman in Boston and with Denman Ross of Harvard University, and has taught at Wellesley College and Harvard. Awarded grants by both the Guggenheim and Ford Foundations, Mr. Bloom has exhibited in one-man shows at the Museum of Modern Art ("Americans 1942"), Institute of Contemporary Art (Boston), Whitney Museum, the Durlacher, Stuart, Boris Mirski, and Swetzoff Galleries, the Venice Biennale, and in group shows throughout the United States and Europe. Collections containing his works include the Museum of Modern Art, Whitney Museum, Fogg Museum (Harvard University), and the Addison Gallery. The Swetzoff Gallery of Boston is agent for Mr. Bloom's drawings; his paintings are handled by the Durlacher Gallery in New York.*

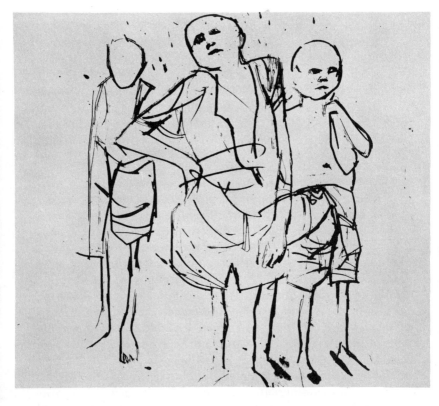

Al Blaustein: *African Boys*. Pen and ink.

28.

Drawings from Life

Al Blaustein

For Al Blaustein drawing does not mean the conventional studio-posed figure — but, rather, the depicting of character in a natural environment. In recent years, Blaustein has taken two trips to Africa, one of them commissioned by the British government for recording life in Tanganyika. "The first drawings produced in Africa," Blaustein commented in his interview, "show the strain of unfamiliar forms, postures, and gestures. It was only toward the end of my year there that I could portray essentials simply and unpretentiously. It took that time to ensure a natural approach — and it takes time before people ignore you sufficiently to ensure observation without intrusion."

In Blaustein's African drawings the subjects were not posed. Nor are the drawings merely swift recordings. They are composed of figures selected from the environment. For example, in *African Boys,* the three figures placed together on one page were in reality far apart from one another when the artist saw them. "Facts were second to feeling," the artist emphasized.

Sidelights of the African trips, which Blaustein recounted, include problems of fear and superstition. Some tribes believe that capturing an image on paper gives the artist power over the souls of those portrayed. "Magic rites" were performed to prevent this. On the other hand, Blaustein found general interest in his work wherever he went. "They passed the drawings from hand to hand, and even though their readings were naturally different, they tried to understand."

At times the trips involved working under peculiar circumstances. "When drawing on the spot," Blaustein continued, "one cannot be pretentious. Technique, or more particularly, *finish,* cannot be considered essential when you are drawing a native dance sequence at night by flashlight." Speed dictates both the instrument and instrumentation. A stick or a straw (with ink) may be the ideal instrument to record movement and gesture under these conditions. If there is no rush, a more customary or traditional technique may be employed. From his ever-present box of pens and ink, the artist might choose one of a variety of flexible steel pen-points.

Blaustein is an artist who constantly draws "out of sheer pleasure," at home, in restaurants, on the subway, as well as on the open road. "The challenge of transforming a white sheet just by drawing a line across it keeps my mind occupied with visual problems." He is not concerned that drawing conceived of as either study or a work in its own right may not be universally appreciated. At a time when *intuition* and *spontaneity* are seemingly prevalent ideas, drawing may not be considered essential or important in preparation for painting. For Blaustein a drawing is primarily a complete and separate work of art. If he uses drawings as a basis for a painting or a print, he does so by pinning up a group of drawings to familiarize himself with the general conception. He does not transfer a specific drawing to canvas or copper. He feels that a rehearsal, which a drawing may also represent, prepares him for a "direct natural attack" based on a thorough knowledge of particular forms and the particular difficulties that may be involved.

If we have given the impression that Blaustein draws essentially on location, it is because his African drawings and those of another trip — through Europe — form a group with consistent themes. But actually he works from memory a great deal. He devotes so much time to drawing that many of the pages he produces are relatively unplanned. He considers these "doodles," as he calls them, to be as valuable as carefully planned works. All of his drawings, which now number in the thousands, make up a file that he consults regularly for stimulation and for neglected ideas.

Al Blaustein: *San Marco,* Pen and ink.

Materials employed by Blaustein are readily available except for a particular paper which he used in Europe. He had been searching for a permanent paper as absorbent as paper napkins or blotters, when an archaeologist in Rome introduced him to "archaeological squeeze paper," which is used in making impressions of bas-reliefs. (It should be noted that this paper is not available commercially.) He is enthusiastic over the surface possibilities of this paper. "San Marco" (page 155), drawn from memory, reveals the staccato-like rhythmical effects which it permits. A more conventional paper which Blaustein frequently employs is "Fabriano Raffaello," which is made in both rough and smooth surfaces. He prefers the "toothy," rough type. Pens employed cover a wide variety of steel points, including lettering pens and a group of Esterbrook fountain pens. Pelikan fountain-pen ink is preferred because of its "rich black which does not clog." Blaustein believes that the conceptual demands of an individual drawing dictate the materials employed, determine the means as well as the approach.

To sum up — Al Blaustein is an artist who draws constantly; his drawings represent a storehouse of form ideas to which he constantly refers. For him the present-day insistence upon *spontaneity* does not diminish the importance of drawing. He considers a drawing a rehearsal, a study of form which may become the basis for translation into another medium, and more important, he also considers a drawing a complete graphic statement.

Born in New York City in 1924, ALFRED BLAUSTEIN *studied at Cooper Union and at present is teaching at Pratt Institute. He has had a one-man show at Nordness Gallery and also has exhibited in group shows at the Metropolitan Museum, Pennsylvania Academy, Albright Gallery, University of Illinois, Carnegie International, Whitney Museum, and elsewhere. His work is included in collections of the Whitney Museum, Library of Congress, and the Everhart Museum (Scranton, Pa.). Mr. Blaustein, who is represented by the Nordness Gallery, received the Priz de Rome, a Guggenheim Fellowship, and a grant from the Institute of Arts and Letters.*